# BIRCHWOOD FARM COMPANY

# "In the Grove"

# 2017

B

F

C

"In the Grove"

"I HAVE NO SPECIAL TALENTS, I AM ONLY
PASSIONATELY *CURIOUS.*" ALBERT EINSTEIN

# COPYRIGHT NOTICE;

# DEDICATION

OUR PURPOSE IN THIS SEPARATES THE TRUE FACTS FROM FICTION;

FIRST AND FOREMOST; IT ALL STARTED IN 1983 WITH EDWARD THE GATEKEEPER WHO POSSESSED AN UNTOLD AMOUNT OF ANTIQUE MINING STOCKS - BOUND IN A BOX AND (**KEPT IN DARKNESS**) IN WHICH TWO OF THESE WERE LATER (**EXPOSED TO LIGHT**).

A GIFT OF INFORMATION IN SCRIPOPHILY FORM WAS GRANTED BY ED. HE CHOSE US AS HIS SUCCESSORS AND "GUARDIANS" AFTER WE PROMISED TO WATCH OVER A RARE PAIR OF "SECRET" STOCKS THAT POINT THE WAY TO REAL PEOPLE AND REAL PLACES.
HE IS ALLOWING FOR A FREE FLOW OF INFORMATION THAT THE STOCKS POSSESS — BELIEVING THAT THEY HAD EDUCATIONAL VALUE BROADENING THE SCOPE OF ENLIGHTENMENT FOR HISTORY'S SAKE. IN SO DOING HE HAS SHOWN THAT HE CARES ABOUT "THE TRUTH."

AFTER WHICH WE EMBARK ON A LONG JOURNEY IN PURSUIT OF KNOWLEDGE - SPANNING 33 YEARS OF STUDY AS NOVICE HISTORIANS IN ORDER TO CONTEMPLATE AND BRING THIS BOOK TO COMPLETION. THE STOCKS ULTIMATELY REVEAL "SECRETS" BY WAY OF SCRIPOPHILY EVIDENCE; THE (**BFC**) LINKS TO A FINANCIAL HISTORY.

SECONDLY; A SPECIAL THANKS TO KATHLEEN; SHE WAS 'BORN THE YEAR' IN WHICH HER "UNCLE BEN" FORMED *BIRCHWOOD FARM* INTO A LEGAL CORPORATION IN 1914.

TO THE OBJECTIVE & INDEPENDENT HISTORIANS IN PURSUIT OF — "THE TRUTH" — THANKS!

"I AM THE WAY, AND "THE TRUTH" AND THE LIFE" JOHN 14; 16

# "WHAT IS PAST IS PROLOGUE"

# CONTENTS

# INTRODUCTION

Opportunely for history's sake a bound pair of stock certificates was found in our hometown following a century of obscurity. The two re-surface and shed light on new evidence in scripophily form that prove invaluable as a primary source. If any mistakes manifest they can be corrected with any subsequent editions. The findings in this are a work in progress, an ongoing research project continuously updated.

BIRCHWOOD FARM GROVE 2017 is an original creation co-authored by us; Vern and Carrie Berg, as a result of a 33-year-meticulous research Quest, the first in-depth study into the Birchwood Farm Co. of Washington. See: ANTIQUE KEEPERS ILLUSTRATED BOOK 2017 is the offshoot of that research, scripophily, and antiquing.

This documented book is validated by our own personal "scripophilist" stockpile. Of these; "two stocks the last of their kind" fit like a jigsaw puzzle." We begin by solving puzzles to complete a clear picture, with torn apart scattered bits and pieces of information. The historical revisionism expressed here is based on our interpretation of events. A wide range of comprehensive material here may contradict conventional history.

Seeking answers to our questions; we embark on a treasure hunt scavenging for clues replete with documents for "historical context." A 'treasury' amassed after compiling tangible objects, newspaper excerpts, first-hand accounts, old magazines, mining certificates, photos, postcards, antique books, stocks, paper relics, and so on.

Of these, two important ascribed paper artifacts kept back in a surreptitious way foreshadow the Reality; of a Hidden Corporation. One of two "secret" stocks was donated for 'safe-keeping' to a cultural (museum) on March 5th 2008.

The First Clue leads to Benjamin Norman, Birchwood's president, a stock Co. A rare pair of "Secret" stocks Numbers 18:19 were issued to James Breen, an adept at smelting and mining. He was eagerly sought-after by "master mining metallurgists."

Of these, included two hotel brothers, "Ben" and "Billy Norman," and a Copper King trio, no less, "William Clark", "Marcus Daly" and Augustus Heinze". We have yet to find the others, the unseen "power elite" shareholders of the company who as a group owned "Birchwood Farm" as their property. The stocks expose "secrets" along the way, and ultimately lead to the financial stock market paradox, causing a bank panic.

Appearances can be deceiving not obvious at first. Under closer scrutiny the stock certificates provide tangible evidence hidden behind a façade of a farmhouse. Ben Norman entertained Friends in the private club under the guise of the Norman Ranch. The "Birchwood Lodge" situated opposite Spokane House, drawing attention away from a tight-knit corporation that you're not supposed to know about. For the most part the company has been largely overlooked by historians. In so doing, they have missed the boat. The fact is, the better-known Hudson's Bay Company (HBC), incorporated in 1670, overshadows the Birchwood Farm Company (BFC).

The two companies were not concurrent. BIRCHWOOD FARM formed into a legal corporation in 1914, organized by the "power of three" trustees as follows; Benjamin Norman, R. E. M. Strickland, and T. B. Higgins. The trio in the midst of tight-lipped pioneer players got in the powerhouse through the back door. Where the best thinkers at the time racked their brains working in the shadows of a farmhouse, historically and tangibly linked financially to Secret Societies, the Spokane Mining Men's Club, (Hotel Spokane Stock Exchange,) Newspapers, Media, Commerce, -Politics, Bohemian Grove, Skull & Bones Society, Knights of the Golden Circle (KGC), the Federal Reserve the (BFC, & WWP) & Real-Estate Land Co's…

Realize that most if not all in this were Freemasons who value "secrecy" above all else, bound together by oaths of protection. (We ourselves are not Freemasons.)

"Masonry, like all the Religions, all the Mysteries, Hermeticism, and Alchemy, conceals its secrets from all except the Adepts and Sages, or the Elect, and uses false explanations and misinterpretations of its symbols to mislead those who deserve only to be mislead; to conceal the Truth, which it calls light, and draw them away from it."
~Morals and Dogma by Albert Pike

**Also since no one has been able to solve the riddle of an elusive stranger;**
In the spring of 2010, the Parks (WSPRC) summoned us to "moonlight" in addition to our ongoing research. After dutifully accepting we shine light that ultimately leads to the identity of a squatter - perpetually bound to a strange iconic building a focal point - identified as the (James "Pea vine Jimmy" Walton threshing barn) presently a tourist attraction - to be found facing the HBC site. The company takes center-stage "surrounded by the Riverside State Park." In place of truth, James Walton has been wrapped in secrecy. No matter how many times a Cliché is repeated for his portrayal of "Pea vine Jimmy" a western cultural icon it still evades the truth. It was as if, no one had searched for him, and nobody knew what became of him. After years of misleading directions in our quest, in the end we track him down. Our final prize "Pea vine Jimmy!" Here and now we reveal James Walton's obscure ORIGIN –ending the misconceptions that describe him. A mythical narrative understates his hidden past. Theirs much more to "Pea vine Jimmy" than what meets the eye!

**Hitherto the research here focuses on new evidence of a hidden history;** Two low profile Innkeepers, James Walton and Benjamin Norman lodge in the same territory at the same time, give or take a few years, upon sacred Native grounds. The "Pea vine Jimmy" threshing barn is just a stone's throw from the "Birchwood Lodge."
Yet, oddly enough, by all accounts these two harbingers did not know one another.

And **stranger still is a distinct character from all those herein mentioned;**
The research in this was no more certain than previous ones. We note "context" for history's sake that may prove useful to "*ripperologists*". While, the cast of true characters reveal certain high–ranking persons herein, they are not to blame. They did however, live concurrent during the multiple murders set in Whitechapel London in 1888. 'Told' in this were Worshipful Masters of a Masonic research Lodge being the first of its kind to study the Masonic Rites and Ceremonies. A few authors have gone so far as to convey that the Lodge in question is implicated in some way. With an endless supply of suspects' and a realm of possible scenarios' the true identity of the killer/killer's may never be known, and has been dubbed "*Jack the Ripper.*"

Lastly **theirs Ed, he let the cat out of the bag with two secret documents;** whilst keeping bound an untold amount of mining stocks in a box. In point of fact: it is a wonder that the duo stocks have survived the test of time. Despite the fact that others have been so long destroyed that not one vestige of them remains.

Two paper relics originate from a sacred place of rituals and fishing, a time of conflict between Native Americans and English colonists, in the midst of the Spokane and Little Spokane rivers, where legendary fishing have long since disappeared.

## Chapter 1
## Hidden Box

It just so happened in Washington State where we live, when a scripophily stockpile was discovered. Of these; two stocks dating back to a century ago sealed our fate. They contain a Holy Grail of information. Our original source of inspiration placed us in a unique position to write the **B**irchwood **F**arm **C**ompany "in the Grove" the first of its kind. How this came about was a calling purely by happenstance.

It has been 33 years since our serendipitous encounter in 1983 with a stranger set in our hometown of Spokane. He suddenly showed up behind us, and at first glance, appeared homeless. We walked with him a ways and engaged in small talk. After which he still seems reluctant to introduce himself. He then stated that he had something of interest to show us. Simply out of curiosity we followed him home.

Before inviting us in, oddly enough he asked, "If we know who the founding father of Spokan is?" Given that my husband and I are local history buffs, the open ended question was a no-brainer. We promptly answered in sync, "James Nettle Glover, one of the true originals and incorporators." A gaze of approval appeared upon Ed's face. He tells us he is a first family descendent of Virginia, and a tale-bearer descended from the Celts. Our ears listened enchantingly to his Celtic mythology and legends. However, enlightening his tales are they seem a bit out of place 'at this time," and are to be continued in our upcoming "Legend & Lore" book.

He then sauntered up a rickety staircase, and came back down holding a chest. After using *a* master key *to* unlock *the box, he told us to c*lose our eyes.

It was at this point, that we "sneak a peek" as he carefully sorted through his treasure trove of untold stocks and minted coins. The moment when we're told to open our eyes he reveals two encapsulated stock certificates – whilst putting the lid back on a hoard of perfectly preserved documents and items of the realm. He then gazes at us with a quirky-wink, as we briefly glimpse mirror images of expired stock.

At this point we find out why the quaint man lured us to his home in the first place.
Keeping us spellbound – "Ed," for the purpose of historical context offers up twin stocks still in pristine condition with stipulations. First and foremost, in no uncertain terms we promise to protect his identity. "Just call me Ed, he said, I'm incognito."

First we made a promise; never to reveal his true name. "We'll never tell." Next, he explained "since the two stocks were found fortuitously, and not by a deliberate search, you can keep one close to you. The other certificate of stock is to be donated "to preserve and protect." He entrusted us as message bearers and protectors of the "secret" stocks with the discretion to choose what to do with the knowledge that they possess. For that reason my husband Vern and I came up with an intriguing and original idea to create a story. We were free from a set of rules, whereas conventional historians are bound to an uncompromising way of thinking.

We were stunned when information comes to light, that these silver and gold mining companies are a direct link to a financial history dating back to a century ago.

Chapter 2

**Secret Stocks**

What happened next after we voluntarily accepted Edward's gift. At this point, his purpose we did not yet understand. "Birchwood Farms" existence was unknown to us, but we would come to know. We suspect as novice historians, he chose us based on our unbiased approach. Since Birchwood Farms inception in 1883 - it would take another one hundred years for the stocks to re-surface. In 1983 as fate would have it we were brought together - where a strange series of events begin to unfold encapsulating an untold story. The doorway of opportunity was opened by an estranged man who hands over from his possession a very unique gift via scripophily. In that way he passed along information for Education purposes and for history's sake. While, it may be true that dead men tell no tales, their possessions left behind can. The research doesn't come easy. We had to decode hidden messages, and think for ourselves, to perceive and interpret real life situations, with real people.

The research herein focuses primarily on two atypical stock certificates; a first hand source of information behind the workings of the BFC. *Two interlocking puzzle pieces* (Numbers 18:19) *fit together, and reveal* surprising new evidence in the form of land scrip. James Breen, a Pacific Northwest "Copper King" was just one of the *rightful title owners of two deeds that entitled him to a piece of "Birchwood Farm," by a conveyance - a* fact that until now has remained a *"secret" that* barely scratches the surface. We are a tiny part of that secrecy beginning with the gift from Ed, a private collector of sorts. His true purpose was to keep close, and keep safe two "secret" stocks, in anticipation of new Stock-keepers. We felt obliged when we took physical possession of the stocks, ending Ed's watch. We were given instructions to protect and return one of the two for preservation. Lo and behold, the Riverside State Park at present has a rightful possession as title holders to a section of "Birchwood Farm" property. Those in the know of said land BFC conveyances' were two cousins, John Binkley and Jacob Taylor, 33rd degree Masons, and practicing attorneys in Roman "Proctor in Admiralty" (Maritime Law) - Wash. Terr. in 1883. [1]

The moment of truth, when the locked box was opened by a "secret stock-keeper" with a skeleton key # 616, exposing "two of a kind" stock certificates. After "vowing to watch" over them, we begin by solving a lot of puzzles, as a test of our knowledge that advanced through further research. Henceforth "a de*fining* moment," and since we are keenly interested in the Bible's perspective on human ideologies, we note; the book of Job in relation to wisdom, a scriptural quotation; Proverbs 16:16 – How much better is it to get wisdom than gold! To get understanding, rather to be chosen than silver! The stocks are worth their weight in gold a genuine Holy-Grail. *There's a story here longing to be told*!

*We've come full circle,* plus the time came to go back to where it all started. But, when we arrive at the place where we've been before, we find the crab apple tree chopped down, and the house Ed lived in no longer standing, with a park in its stead. We made a promise, and could not, in good conscience, back out of our deal.

## Chapter 3
## The Obligatory Research Curse Begins

A number of "secret" stocks were bound and kept in an attic. When the right time elapsed two of these were pulled from darkness, back into the light. Edward persuaded us to guard them. After which we made a promise to look after them.

To fulfill our writing obligations, we've since withheld his name… excepting his first name and initials, E. T. (we kid you not).

Like super-sleuths we worked hard to crack the puzzles following the back stories where the stocks lead. Thus far, our important contribution of researching the stocks secrets, have been ignored, whilst "we've been throwing clues out there" since our first manuscript in 1989. Speaking in scripophily terms, the stocks possess historical information. We endlessly took notes to put into proper perspective the ideas that kept "pouring in."

Mulling over the odd arrangement only adds to the mystery. For instance; who gave Ed, the encapsulated stocks in the first place, only to be opened a century later? We imagine that Ed, a man of secrecy practiced as a corporate or private attorney. At the time of this writing, the reality is that the public is continually being inundated with fake news. As a result, more think tanks are popping up, to educate the public, on how to spot - fake news. Inviting an obvious question; "who will spot the "fake news-spotters?" In other words; "Who is watching the Watchmen"?

Since, historical narratives of the Old Spokane House have been documented elsewhere; a summary of events mixed with new knowledge may suffice. The secret stocks point the way to real people and real places, a cultural heritage of historical significance. Of a subject matter into the financial workings of linked companies herein, many of which were doing business during the worldwide depressions of epic proportions in U. S. history. They add educational insight of historical significance exposing truths along the way, which lead to historical paradoxes.

An obligatory research curse was to follow Ed's gift. A pivotal moment possessed by free will, but literally bound in a constrained manner with a series of research projects each one leading into the next. Without that research our work would never be brought to completion. Bound by a labor of love, we have endured long hours of reading, research, headaches, typing, writer's calluses, cramps, and so on - a direct result of suffering from the curse. In a sense, our most treasured possessions attached an imprint of energy residue left behind. There *was* no easy way to lift the curse, apart from a Knowledge Quest and the parting of many beloved antiques. To put all this behind us we tried hard to unlock our hidden potential, and become familiar with with our inquisitive character. But first, we must re-visit a Sacred Space where the transfer of residual left-over energy of emotionally charged life changing events has happened. Figuratively the "secret" stocks uncover clues that lead to "Birchwood," a company that we've never heard of, leaving us in the dark until further research. The Birchwood Farm Company leads the way directly across the road to the enigmatic "James "Pea vine Jimmy" Threshing Barn.

Next, the scavenger hunt grows wider when we follow the trail that connects to the former **H**udson's **B**ay fur-trading **Co**. As local Spokane history buffs the HBC was a familiar company we have heard of, a familiar place. The clues begin to manifest automatically in which we already know; then we write an overview of the *Hudson's Bay Company;* King Charles II of England founded in November 1660 – then granted on May 2nd 1670 the Royal Charter; an exclusive trading monopoly. The Old Spokane House established as a fur trading post over a century later in 1810, under David Thompson's supervision, an associate of the North-West Fur Trading Co. Spokane House was the *first* settlement of white men to settle here. Jacques (Jaco) Finlay, a Metis, and Finnan McDonald were left in charge by David Thompson. Spokane House saw a rivalry between 1810-1826 w/ the North-West Fur Co. which built a few buildings at the site in 1810 - the Pacific Fur Co. owned by John Jacob Astor - and that of the Hudson's Bay Co.

**Spokan Chief Garry** was born circa 1811 on his ancestral native homeland, at the confluence of the Spokane and the Little Spokane Rivers. John Clark was left in charge setting up their post buildings in 1812 adjacent to the NWC establishing their fur companies and friendly rival posts nearby. After the war of 1812 the NWC bought out Astor's Company in 1813 later merging with the HBC in 1821. Spokane House later re-moved in 1826 to Fort Spokane aka Spokane House. Jaco Finlay remained at Spokane House until his death apparently about 1829. The Spokane House land passed from Great Britain and became United States Territory first in 1846 settling the boundary between them. This was confirmed so by Emperor 1 of Germany in 1873 after settling a border dispute between these two countries.

Isaac Ingalls Stevens (1818–1862), an Indian agent was the *first* Territorial Governor of the state of Washington who stopped at the junction of two rivers, in 1853-54 to survey the area for the N.P.R.R. He is a cousin of Laura Ingalls Wilder, a descendent from John Stevens from the first families who arrived in Andover, Salem Village Massachusetts.

As luck would have it, in 1658 the settler's were made to witness the violent witch-hunt during the colonial settlements. The Rev., Cotton Mather along with selectmen preached through conviction that witches and demons were living in the midst of the local residents.

Mary Parker was executed in 1692 among others in the Salem witch trials and her daughter Sarah Parker was later accused. Mary Parker, is the 8th great-grandmother of U.S. President George W. Bush, who descends from 217 trial victims. Sarah Jessica Parker, an actress, is a descendent of Mary Parker.

In due course; the United States of America granted lands to the N.P.R.R. Railroad Corporation - passed and approved by Congress on July 2nd, 1864.

In 1881 the Northern Pacific Railroad was completed to the east end of the pacific coast in 1883. By train supplies could now be transported to and from the east coast to the Pacific Northwest, resulting in new settlers to the Washington Territory.

Chapter 4
**If an old Stock could Talk**

The binding of two century old stock certificates kept secrets in the dark. It behooves us to go into the dark to find an intuitive grasp of the truth, to make public a small part of that secrecy. The two were "worth guarding" they prove no match *for* an untold part of history, which should have been told years ago.

From a fresh perspective as "outside writer's who think outside the box" we pay a visit in 1983 to Spokane House to bind our story with intuitive insight.  When we arrive to the (park) we follow along familiar trails that lead to an ancient grove, where we spot all kinds of creatures inhabiting the tall cottonwoods.  An ancient way traveled by the indigenous peoples of the Spokane and other Native tribes, a sacred place where they had been meeting for centuries thriving on fishing, foraging and hunting, at a place overflowing with "legendary King Chinook Salmon" spawning in their natural habitat along the river currents of the Spokane and the little Spokane Rivers - by way of a natural selection of evolution "long before" the war of the currents - between competing electric power companies evolution spanning the late 1880s and the early 1890s – that caused a paradigm shift in the Natives livelihood".

This is how the story goes, a familiar history where "Pea vine Jimmy", squatted on the threshing-floor of a strange building at the old Spokane House in the late-1870s, now recognized as the James (Pea vine Jimmy) Walton Threshing barn, a familiar place, a sacred space nearby the "Y" where "the Spokane and Little Spokane Rivers meet," the present Spokane House Interpretive Center joining the "wye" to an unfamiliar place where Ben Norman settled at "Birchwood" in 1883 and built the "BFC Lodge" forming a triangle where 'at the time' no territorial boundary in Washington State existed between one another.  The historical site provides a safe rookery for the Great Blue Heron, where two harbingers of spring Ben' and James' lived opposite the other in an isolated community *unaware from one another* – where the two must remain tethered to the old fur-trading post, "trapped by history."

To tell our story with certainty we examine closely from our private collection of antiques.  The clarity we seek becomes even clearer after touching, smelling and feeling two "secret" stocks, during contemplation.  We have had 33 years to enlighten ourselves, but worth the wait, the "text" in this is different than any heard to date.

The stock certificate #18 emerges as the mirror image (of #19), ephemera attached in some way to a sacred site.  The two paper artifacts, abstract reflections begin manifesting disturbing imagery of a shadow history, conveying new levels of truth.  After which we are beset with precocious intellect, a strong sense of "ominous dark clouds gathering overhead." Bold Iconic American metaphors draw a closer reading of "manifest destiny". When once more it seems, *history repeats itself*, raising uncomfortable issues. Metaphorically the stocks speak loudly and clearly in scripophily form evoking feelings in times past – by way of sensory perception in our memory banks that depict a fixed image of an American flag, a symbol of freedom.

According to our estimation, we can reasonably expect that James Walton arrived to the Washington Territory in the early-1870s, where he meets his merchant friends in Colville. In 1882 he settles in Chattaroy nearby the Little Spokane River where the mouth opens at Dragoon Creek. Dragoon translated literally from French, means "French dragon," from Latin, "draconarius" or Old French (Draco).

Spring was in the air "mingled with the scent of a cool ocean breeze" many travelers and emigrants had left their homeland for America, from the Liverpool port in mid-Victorian England. Benjamin Norman in May of 1882 sailed from this point forward crossing the Atlantic, arriving in the U.S. (7-10) days later.
See; (Immigration Act of 1882)

Ben, a stocky Englishman of Saxon descent and ancient Norman stock soon discovers, that the historic HBC lands he settled upon was in possession by Native Americans. A ritual site used tribally for centuries, for the purpose of gathering medicines, berries, and vegetation. The various tribes gathered here and danced in practice of their first ceremonies and spiritual beliefs – the first spring Chinook salmon caught each year beginning with the first-salmon ceremonies. A favorite hunting and fishing spot where the Spokane and the Little Spokane Rivers join. [2]

Historically speaking, Mr. Norman is the first on record to purchase 590 acres of farm land, here from the largest real estate owner the N.P.R.R. in 1883.

Following the land purchase in a *celebratory mood* three immigrant newcomers from England; Benjamin Norman, Bishop Daniel Sylvester Tuttle and the Rev. Charles Compton Burnett go on a camping and fishing trip in the summer of 83. At best they chose a spot of land nearby the old fur trading post, a sacred site at the junction of the Spokan and Little Spokan Rivers. After a day of fishing and eating their fill of legendary King Chinook salmon, cooked over an open fire, what might these three pioneers' have talked about before bed, while staring at the stars that night?  Ben may have read from the book; Astoria Enterprise beyond the Rocky Mountains by Washington Irving (1783–1859), a friend of John Jacob Astor who gave a detailed account of the adventurers among the Native tribes, fur traders and the events to follow?  The British gentlemen's camping spot still had the aura of a wild encampment?  After all, Native tribes were still in the area, one of their favorite places to spear and cure fish.  But, when the settlers begin taking Native lands, various tribes get caught in the middle, this spells trouble.  In the way of progress control of the sacred grove was one of many territories taken by way of military conquest and treaties marking 'a turning point' of conflicting events between the European settlers and the Natives.

Conflict was widespread among the early settlers, farmers and the miners who crept over sacred spaces, where the *i*ndigenous peoples were forcibly removed to reservations.  The "right of conquest," shifts the balance of power and influences history.  The horses carried "the others" strangers to an unknown land.  The emigrants would rather face the Natives, and risk dangers they did not yet understand, rather than return to their homeland of oppression from whence they came.  They were looking for a place of their own, a place they could call home.  Many emigrants were Quakers from (the Religious Society of **Friends**), Huguenots, and various oppressed sects united with exiled missionaries, in search of religious freedom.

We get it, but the place they chose was already inhabited, the very same place where "the very same thing happens to Chief Garry," who lived life free on open territory up until the time of conflict.  And in turn, he is exiled from the land of his birth" - where time crept peacefully for the original inhabitants.  "The spell of calm" before the storm of military soldiers assimilated Native tribes from their motherland to reservations.

The native peoples faced insurmountable odds between adversarial relations.  Inevitably Chief Garry anxiously watched events play out in the way of progress and change. Inescapably caught in a no win situation - in which case he did not win. In one heart wrenching scenario; when Col. George Wright took revenge against the Natives including the Coeur d'Alene, Spokane and the Palouse tribes, and the horses they kept. Company soldiers were sent to slaughter the horses and destroy the shelters and feed lodges kept for both the horses and the Natives.

Hundreds of horses were made to suffer the after effects; due to the "right of conquest; the right of a conqueror to territory, "land" taken by force of arms, and owing to the "humiliation Colonel Steptoe suffered in 1858, in his defeat with the Natives. The slaying of horses happened nearby the Spokane River. The Native horses were made to suffer a horse sacrifice, a slow agonizing ritual of death, where the horses anxiously awaited two long autumn days for their turn to "give up the ghost." A mass horse burial of bones remains aka "Horse Slaughter Camp." The horses were a vital part of the Natives ancient culture and livelihood. *"It is what it is."* [3]

The Federal Government prevented the Natives from hunting and fishing on their old grounds of seemingly endless territories. In 1882 the law forbids the Native Americans from practicing ritual ceremonies on sacred spaces.

Ben Norman became a naturalized citizen on Dec. 27th 1883 in Cheney, Washington. Natives were not granted U. S. citizenship Until the Indian Citizenship Act of 1924. [4]

After the conquest; and the end result of the Spokane "Shanty-town case used the "severance damages rule" See; (Enoch v. Spokane Falls & N. Ry. Co. 1893*)* the land promised to Enoch was put in possession of Benjamin son of George Norman.

The shift from ancient Native land had been replaced with "Birchwood Farm," where the freemasons affiliated with the private "Norman Lodge" who in turn began practicing Masonic rituals in 1883, on a tract of land that was once used by the original inhabitants, who practiced their ancient rituals on sacred ground here.

Ceremonials to Bring Spirit Help; Villages and tribes used dances and other ceremonials to seek spirit help. In general, the men conducted these activities. Usually they had a house where secret societies met, and sacred ritual objects were kept. Ceremonials were taught to the young. ~ Enoch

"In the 1880's the salmon ran thick in both the Little Spokane and Spokane Rivers. During the salmon season although the Indian Reservation had been created an effort was made to force the Indians onto the reservation. The Indians still maintained fish traps across the little Spokane river and main Spokane River. There were 25-35 tepees [150-185 Native Americans] during the salmon season. Major Simms and Major O' Neal of the Colville Indian Agency made constant efforts to get the Indians to move onto the reservation and the Indian tepees and salmon traps were destroyed in an effort to force the Indians to leave the spot. "I recall some trouble over the Indian fish traps. The Indian had a number of these traps. Some two or three were on Ben Norman's place and two or three on my fathers place. The early settler's including the people at Spokane Falls, demanded that the Indians close their fish traps at least once a week to permit some of the fish to go upstream as some of their traps caught virtually every fish that came along. When the Indians forgot to close their traps one day a week, a party of settlers interested in fishing, including that of John Dickinson Sherwood, Benjamin Norman and the others came to the traps and tore out two or three of them. Later the Indian Agent tore out the remaining traps in an effort to force the Indians to quit the spot and move onto the Indian Reservation. There were so many fish during the fishing season that no one except some of the old timers who actually saw the fish, would believe me if I attempted to tell you about it. The fish were actually so numerous that it was no sport whatever to catch them. The Indians caught them and smoked them by the ton." ~ End of statement; Rev. P. Burnett

Sidney D. Waters, Indian Agent (W. T.) wrote a letter on June 7th 1884, to the Colville Indian Agency; on Benjamin Norman's behalf. Mr. Norman stated that he bought the Land in question from the Railroad Company (copy enclosed) at the mouth of the Spokane and the Little Spokane Rivers, where four Natives, John Stevens, Simon and Jeremiah had been trap fishing. It was the scene of the "conflict" over the overuse of "fish traps," resulting from the clashes between the "early settler's" and the "various Native tribes." In the end the Native's were fined and jailed for it. Rev. C. Compton Burnett and G. H. Belden paid the Natives an enumeration of $110 for crops that they had planted prior to the whites being there. The claim of John Stevens could not be settled on account of the absence of Norman. The traditional fish traps caused a culture shock among the settler's, who found the use of fish traps strange. [5]

For the elite a sense of beauty and splendor evokes feelings of the gilded age until the great fire in 1889. When they had no place to stay the Norman bros. Ben and Billy open their doors to the Hotel Spokane that same year and come out "smelling like money." King Chinook salmon, Green turtle consommé and frogs fresh from the little Spokane River, were served on the menu at the Hotel Spokane Silver Grill.

In 1889 Ben Norman purchased 160 acres in the Indian Trails Five Mile Area in Spokane, where J. D. Sherwood purchased land one year earlier. [6]

The European settlers were able to purchase land here as a result of the 1820 Land Act "manifest destiny" in America, which was good for the wealthy capitalists and or the early settlers who could afford the lower cost land. However it increased the confiscation of Indian land from the Native Americans.

'Lastly, the sacred land was colonized and the lands change hands many times over'.

Chief Garry's early years were spent in a land of "milk and honey" but his later years were spent in poverty - on the breadline, so to speak. In the end he died about 1892 - 'a parallel time,' when the Spokane Mining exchange and Chamber of Commerce "money-men" began their business meetings in the Hotel Spokane. [7]

In 1905 W. S. Norman, a co-owner of the Hotel Spokane was "caught red-handed" from deer poaching during the month of January. As a consequence he was found guilty in police court to having venison in his possession, killed out of season.  He was fined one dollar, in his defense William claimed the game was shot in Idaho. [8]

## SUFFERIN' CODFISH HE'S GOT ME BEAT COMPLEAT ANGLER

BEN NORMAN
On the Banks of the Spokane

Ben Norman in caricature form fishing on the banks of the Spokane River, above Spokane Falls, nearby the Edison Electric Illuminating Co. Power House in 1910 – whilst "IKE WALTON" hovers over him in the form of a ghost."  Was William C. Morris (1874-1940), a Spokesman Review Cartoonist inserting "secret" messages in cartoons?  Subliminal clues that may be revealing James "Pea vine Jimmy" Walton is related to Izaak Walton (1594–1683)?

In 1914 'Birchwood Farm' legally incorporated.  The ownership was through the equity "stock" of its owner's (stockholders) – a small group of money men who still control much of our resources today as they did yesterday.  Corporations and banks regulate the currency.  The

BFC and the HBC were not concurrent – but the two companies situated nearby the little Spokane river bank – controlled by currents. Rivers - banks regulate currency controlled by a "money flow" - to the financial markets trickle-down effect – to significant events that play out herein described. In commerce the "pioneer power players" had an overall effect on the stock exchange.

Ben Norman remained the B. F. Company president until his passing in 1934. That same year "the company" was stricken and dissolved from the records by the Secretary of State - and the Riverside State Park was born. The (park) is managed by The Washington State (Parks) and Recreation Commission (WSPRC), where the Spokane House Interpretive Center exhibits the Spokane Natives, early pioneers, and the old Spokane House fur trading post. The (park) was mainly created by members of the Civilian Conservation Corps (CCC) and gifts of land in 1933-34. Effectively through foresight by Aubrey Lee White and Burgess Lee Gordon, and a few other innovative locals who 'acted in concert," via corporations like the (CCC) and the Washington Water Power Company (WWPC) who donated the land. B. L. Gordon additionally helped in the planning of the Grand Coulee Dam. The Spokane Fish Hatchery located on Glen Tana Farm, Waikiki Rd. began in 1903 partly by a few local Spokane capitalists and Dr. B. L. Gordon. The latter additionally controlled a trout pond, near Penrith, Newport, Wash. Where he contemplated the idea to install an electric gas powered light plant on his private property for personal use, and to light the rural community where a select few intended to build their summer homes. [9]

The lack of hindsight in the development of the many hydropower dams, and the lack of fish-ladders had enormous consequences, a far-reaching ripple effect. The Chief Joseph Dam completely blocked salmon migration, including that of the fresh water eel to the upper Columbia River. As a result the fish suffered the ill effect, which has a negative karmic effect in the end. That negative energy in turn affected not only the early Settler's, but most especially Native American families' whose livelihood depended upon the fish-traps, and the drying of fish, during lean times.

The "Karma trap" after effects set against the Natives were utterly appalling.

The irony of the story is that in the end, "all good things must come to an end". The fish decline was not the cause of drying of fish, and fish-traps, "an ancient tradition." As you might expect, after the upheaval the transition period to progress nowadays the generational hereditary legendary fish have since been eliminated, and are now genetically engineered. Today the fish are grown in over-crowded concrete ponds and stock tanks. Fish farmers control whole artificial ecosystems, providing everything necessary for the fresh water fish to reproduce before release.

Follow the money trail that leads to currency trickling down the river - banks to sacred grounds to the disturbing descriptions of events. Still due, owing to the technology of hydropower development, canneries, overfishing and pollution, many species of fish today are still suffering from the ripple effects through the currents, such as the fresh water eel.

In effect the Power-Players would soon have some explaining to do. Some of the main players linked along the power lines based on the direct current of DC/ AC of the Edison Electric Light Company.

(William Norman signed the (WWPC) articles of incorporation on March 13, 1889; along with 9 other investors. Including William's brother in-law Frank Rockwood Moore, WWP 1st pres., John Dickinson Sherwood, J. W. Chapman, J. P. M. Richards, Daniel Chase Corbin (1832-1918), Cyrus R. Burnes, William Pettet, H. Bolster, and J. Prickett).
See: the Illuminati-ng Co.

"If you want to find the secrets of the universe, think in terms of energy, frequency and vibration." – Nikola Tesla

Chapter 5
**Our quest-after James "Pea vine Jimmy" Walton**

Our first independent research began in 1983 following a chance discovery of two BFC stock certificates. The Recreation and Conservation Office (RCO) are responsible for thousands of historical objects. Now add to that list; one of two paper artifacts (# 19) that we hand delivered in person to a Washington State Park Ranger. The purpose of which, was a gift, a donation to the RCO to share in support of the Washington state (parks), and to continue a free-flow of information for "historical context" of archeological sites. It seemed fitting at the time, since the paper relics go full circle back to where they were created.

Our next research project *began* when we were summoned to bring into the light a familiar; known as "Pea vine Jimmy" whose origin has been cloaked in mystery for some time now. The Washington State Parks wrote us a letter, dated March 09, 2010, thanking us for our persistent research. This is before common or public knowledge into James "Pea vine Jimmy" Walton's genealogy and real identity! "They" thought that "Pea vine Jimmy" sounded like an interesting character, and it would be fun to learn more about him. In addition to our former obligations 'at the time' we were unable to recognize any preconceived notions of the outcome that another research project would entail. After answering the call we began our second research project as anonymous author's, to help the (Parks), obliged for history's sake. (We were not on the payroll). We begin by *acting* like super-sleuths on a quest to gather information in our attempt to track him down. We re-examined any "cryptic clues" left behind, but to no avail. In view of this we became suspicious. Questions arose having the earmarks of his origin being shielded from public view – "even still" suggestive of being methodically downplayed." His true character a closed book has been mixed with folklore to create a western frontiersman – masking his true identity.

When we get to close to the truth, we are beset by forces that "cast shadows" throwing us off course. Did his friends cast doubt, egregiously enabling him to stay under the radar – even before and after his death? Determined to fulfill our end of the bargain and protect the "secret" stocks – we stayed hot on his trail and tracked down clues that ultimately lead to historical details of his life. A much bigger challenge was lurking ahead. To create and re-write a new story that nobody's ever read before.

We looked hard in search of documents in relation to James Walton, as we had done for Benjamin Norman.  In so doing, makes the past more extensive for "historical context."  In pursuit of knowledge new doors were opened, whilst closes doors as well.  Whereas official historians and historical pioneer societies are privy to archival documents early on, personal interviews and primary sources.  As "independent historians" our research was challenged given the lack of resources.

There were times when our questions were circumvented, making the research harder along the way.  An image of James Walton remains to be seen.  Maybe someday soon one will come crawling out of the woodwork?  We came close to seeing a photo likeness of James Walton, but a Historical Museum in Ohio ignored our written request.  Questions arise was there a possible conflict-of-interest, relative to the staff member who is in a position to benefit monetarily and or notoriety?"

Our intent all along has been to publicly share and declare for the first time a personal photo of James's likeness of his physical appearance.  In spite of any indications to the contrary, "Pea vine Jimmy" remains an American iconic figure in our history – hence the building "monument" so named in his honor.

James Walton supervised the biggest mines, yet his identity had remained hidden behind mining corps.  B. Norman and J. Walton were heavily invested in mining.  The two shared similar ideals in freemasonry deeply rooted within their families.  Was James Walton known only to a mere handful, couple with (B. Norman, G. B. Ide, and B. F. Goodman), privy to information early on within the 'inner circles' of the brotherhood the illuminati?  The freemason's secret societies activities, events and inner functioning are concealed from non-members or to outsiders.  His identity may have been kept secret and known only to an initiated few – a secret that has been kept hidden for years.  James' background has been vague – that is until now.  In which case, we have attempted to fill in some of the blanks of our subject with a brief biographical sketch insofar as we know, and reveal his true identity.

Is there anything new to learn from two century old (*stocks*) paper relics? We began to wonder if our interest was unwarranted. Previous historians have been studying for decades the HBC archeological site. But, something was amiss; no indication of how James Walton arrived to the Wash. Terr., his parentage, and or the circumstances of his birth and death has ever been explained. The historian Jonathan Edwards's account only marginalizes details of him. Therefore we had no idea his true identity existed outside the fictitious character *"Pea vine Jimmy."*

That is odd, given the fact that the enigmatic "Pea vine Jimmy" building enclosed within the state park receives particular public attention. Apparently his background has been so well hidden, that it has even eluded the understanding of historians and scholars alike, including those in charge of the local historical societies, and that of family members who "are expected to know." The fact on the face of it not yet fully researched or discovered? The "Pea vine Jimmy" myth may have overshadowed historical details of his life. We begin with a close-reading of books in search of clues that the previous historians may have missed. The atypical suppositions commonly accepted about him are full of holes. Vigorous perspicacity allowed us to see right through them. By no means did we uncover his true-story overnight slowly but surely it came into view.

James' lived over a century ago, we *delve* more *deeply into the sources* available to strip away decades of myth and misconceptions to reveal the identity of an elusive stranger. A conspiracy view herein was never the writer's intention. If truth be told – sometimes the truth is stranger than fiction.

All things considered, we have worked very hard on simultaneous research projects at the same time, 33 years of cumulative research.

We looked for answers scrutinizing over obfuscated etymological origins, onomastics and methodology. Our intent has been to severe fact from fiction. Unraveling the myth behind "Pea vine Jimmy" may sound controversial at first. A re-interpretation of real-life events adds to the historical record. Biological and historical roots give way to distinctive

characteristics of "Pea vine Jimmy" adding "veins" by means of his "bloodline relatives," his real-life story is an eye-opener.
A hidden "clinging grapevine" that was ripe for the picking.

# CHAPTER 6
## THE BUILDING ENIGMA

We have called into question both the strange building and the unknowable builder. For what it's worth, we've added our two cents to the "research quest". As "outsiders" looking into the Historical Societies text, we take a shot at; and try to find the answers; to better describe James' character, and mysterious background.

The official historians; have unconstrained access to the same primary sources, yet oddly enough have repeated diverse interpretations of the same event. Thus far, they have been unable to solve the "Pea vine Jimmy" riddle of the strange squatter, allegedly connected with the strange building."

As of this writing, we are subjecting these muddled facts to revision, after a closer examination of two secret stocks that contain scripophily knowledge." They "bring into the light" new information in the company of meticulous importance, due to the position of the enigmatic building sited nearby the familiar Hudson Bay Company and that of the unfamiliar Birchwood Farm Company. That is where we come in, to help sort out the facts, which have basically been reduced to muddles.

The new evidence pierces the building enigma and "Pea vine Jimmy lore" that has likely shrouded the truth about the building's origin and that of its builder. This does little to venerate James Walton's true identity. He is mostly remembered by the (parks) visitors for the double - pen log building he allegedly left behind. Our revision of events may beg to differ with the typical version side of the story. Before we begin, were going to bring you up to speed with THE STORY thus far; a simple explanation that James "Pea vine Jimmy" Walton built the building, recognized by a consensus as the second oldest log structure in Spokane County.

*Strangely enough, an account of James Walton has never been recorded.*

**The time of *revelation* to the *identity* of the builder/ builder's is overdue;** Found at last; James Walton's *Friends, "*Frank Goodman and Jacob Stitzel." The two are among the creators of the Stevens County Pioneer Association in Colville on Oct. 1, 1903 aka the Stevens County Historical Society. The latter of the two, was an appraiser, Fort Colville, as of Aug. 6th 1897, Appraiser, Fort Colville. [10]

Thus far, the historians seemingly remain vague and unconcerned about James Walton's origin. No rhyme or reason; having no merit putting together the missing pieces of the puzzle. The "historical text" is ambiguous with varying versions of events and conflicting idea's (ideates) on whether or not it was built by Natives, or "Pea vine Jimmy"? At present; the said building is named in honor of James "Pea vine Jimmy" Walton (origin unknown) the sacred site occupied previously by various Native tribes, and the HBC. The tourists who visit the park are intrigued by the legend of "Pea vine Jimmy" and the mysterious building.

The official historians; have debated over the building's origin, whilst having seemingly had little interest in the builder's origin. The (Parks) summoned us in 2010 to search for James "Pea vine Jimmy" Walton. So far the building has remained an enigma, even to those historians who have been studying it for many years.
To date very little is known about James' he remains a true mystery.

Furthermore, no matter how much evidence we "bring to the table" we anticipate some skepticism along the way, which no doubt will add our revision of events to any other existing controversies.

As of this writing, the official version of the building/ buildings still has unfounded accounts, not sufficiently grounded in fact. They are not absolutely certain of whom the builder is or the builders are. Due to scarce and scattered information, conflicting ideas, as to the events, exact names, dates, and purpose of the building/ buildings, the subject remains a matter of debate. Interpretations vary as to who built the bldg, the Natives, a Settler or Settler's?

The burden of proof is on the historian/ historian's who made the claim. In this case conjectures are vaguely based upon, Edward T. Becher a local historian, author, freemason and an "authority," on the subject. He first theorized in relation to the building, that Native Americans built it between the' 1850s - 60s - for the purpose of storing hay, and or grain. Secondly, Mr. Becher claimed a "squatter" built the building in the late 1870's. "If that is the case then (Enoch 1870's) may well have built the bldg. – if it had indeed been built in the 1850's as Becher first theorized.

"In the 1850s Benjamin F. Yantis was implicated in Wash, Terr., politics, as Captain of the civilian militia group the 'Spokane Invincibles,' (1857 Indian War). The word Invincible is a Latin verb vincere, 'to conquer.' Bechers first theory dates the bldg. to the 1850s period of armed warfare, Yantis-1850's-Chief Garry's mill." [11]

**From that point forward, according to the official historical accounts;** from the late-1870s a squatter built the log building where the Spokane River and Little Spokane River meet at Spokane House, (old fur trading post) founded in 1810). The squatter/ supplanter remains tethered to the earthly remains of the building presently recognized as the James "Pea vine Jimmy" Walton threshing barn – surrounded within the Riverside State Park's perimeter, below Nine Mile Falls Dam, and along N. Nine Mile Rd. Outdoor markers lead the way along clear paths to follow and signposts to show the way. As you walk along the trails around the "Pea vine Jimmy Threshing barn" keep in mind, that the building merits a great deal of attention, whilst little is known of the building and that of its builder.

The conventional belief that James built the bldg. is raised into question; if one believes the theory that the building was single-handedly built by James. Until the story is proved untrue – either way, there is no certainty that James "Pea vine Jimmy" Walton built the building, and no certainty that he did not. The lack of answers only makes the building more intriguing – and a matter of debate among historians. To obscure and complicate matters further, adding mystification - James Walton's back-story has been absorbed into a code name on the public record, aka "Pea vine Jimmy."

The way we picture it, the surviving evidence is too vague to lead to a consensus. On the other hand, we can throw some truth into the mix, putting a slightly different slant on the details.

We have tried hard to come up with some new evidence, and throw away the old clichés. We challenge the notion; that if James' did indeed build the building, then he may have had a little help from his merchant Friends and stage coach partners in doing so - based on our study of groundbreaking research and documents that reveal a hidden truth, a paradox is at odds with the present version of events.

In historiography, the term historical revisionism identifies with the re-interpretation of the historical record compared with the views held by previous scholars about a historical event. As local history buffs we came across some of these earlier historical accounts. After we unearthed more current documented sources beginning w/ "secret" stocks our historical revisionism may in some ways contrast with the more familiar "context." In isolation, may read akin to "alternative" history.

We try to better explain what happened, and why it happened that way without self-censorship, based upon our discretion rather than by conventional wisdom.

By all accounts the stories of days past told in Benjamin Norman's words; is repeatedly told by the Burnett Bros. Curiously, of the accounts herein; most of which did not have the foggiest idea who "Pea vine

Jimmy" was? However, conveniently they all knew each other in this tightly-knit area of Nine Mile Falls, Spokane County. Recounts from Charles C. Burnett's sons Hugh and Oswald follow along a similar line of Ben Norman's; - details of the building vary little. They never disclose personal information about him. Whether or not they knew of him is unclear, either intentionally or unintentionally. Most if not all were members or Friends and or family to each other. The stories of James "Pea vine Jimmy" Walton parallels between the lives of the other Quakers living in the tight-lipped community Chattaroy, Spokane County. Our point being; in the midst of Quakers, Robert P. Cowgill lived in the same territory at the same time of James Walton. Mr. Cowgill had similar interests as that of James Walton. Robert acted as a Judge, mining, a farmer, and merchant, operating a dry goods store in Chattaroy in 1883-1895, and later resigned as Post Master in 1889, when Flora A. Langst became Post Mistress in 1889. Fraternally Mr. Cowgill was a charter member of the Odd Fellows (I. O. O. F.) and the Knights of the Maccabees (*K. O. T. F.)* See: Jacobite rising of 1745.

The Burnett "bros" Hugh and Oswald, surmised that the building/ buildings; were associated with a roadhouse Tavern on the old Colville Road built dating back to the 1840s -1850s, "Peavine Jimmy," never comes to mind. They did however make mention of the described barn and other buildings, in which he learned that the roadhouse was probably erected by a character named *Frenchman Bone.*"

Incidentally, "Frenchman Bone's" story runs parallel with that of "Pea vine Jimmy". The following brief excerpt an account of "Frenchman Bone" recorded by William S. Lewis as an employee of the (HBC) a Fur Trader - 1810. His son was George Heron born in 1834, at Fort Nisqually near Olympia, his mother a Colville Native. To make a long story short, George mentions a character known as 'Frenchman Bone', a Metis mail carrier who built a roadhouse near the mouth of the Little Spokane River. Curiously, Lewis never recorded an account for James "Pea vine Jimmy" Walton. [12]

Fred A. H. Culverwell, an Advisory board member of the Washington -State Historical Records was an authority on the subject. After studying the history of Spokane House for many years, he came to varying conclusions contradictory to the accepted ones. For instance; he disputed the location of the main bldg. [13]

**The Northern Pacific Railroad;** reported during their survey the following;
"This building stood farther to the west near the woods in 1885, left incomplete with no roof by an unknown squatter. The logs were carefully numbered and moved over near the present ranch buildings, and then put together again. We fixed it up and used it for sleeping quarters. When B. L. Gordon bought the place in 1912 he moved it to its present position. Gordon believed it had some historical value and was not pleased when told it was of no importance." ~ The statement relative to the old log building; was made by Oswald Burnett to the writer on April 14, 1946. [14]

In 1884-85 Benjamin Norman was the owner of the Spokane Tent Company. The survey crew 'at the time' could have slept in tents if they so desired. [15]

Enoch lived concurrently on said section of land during the same time, as "Pea vine Jimmy." It's remotely possible that "Enoch" built the said building. After all, he was promised a section of N.P.R.R. Railroad land, at the mouth of the little Spokane River after losing his land (Spokane downtown shanty case.) [16]

At various times the logs were reused for fires and new buildings. It is not without reason when one looks at the old log building which is inaccessible for human access, but ideal for animal quarters, or for the purpose of drying hay. This is not to say that the building didn't have various uses at different times. To help clear up any confusion – we've requested any photo evidence ascertained from the archeological site (circa 1934). Any remains of the bldg and or buildings left behind, in all likelihood were documented, along with the 'Singumanish Farms,' sign allegedly hung at B. L. Gordon's property. "A picture would be worth a thousand words."

**Based on the brief excerpt from the N.P.R.R. report our opinion is;**

"Perhaps the old log building was re-used later as a double crib-barn for two log pens for the purpose of small livestock. Dr. B. L. Gordon did raise livestock and pigs here. SINGUMANISH LADY was furrowed March 12, 1918 - a litter of boars and sows - bred by A. H. Poston & Sons, of Spokane, and sold to Mr. Gordon." (Mrs. Poston named the pigs Singumanish). It was not until recently that the name "Singumanish" has been given hieroglyphics; making it a Spokan Native name. [17]

If the building was indeed built by "Pea vine Jimmy" as alleged in the late 1870s (Becher's theory), then the condition of the building's appearance would be good, as a result of only being a decade old, "give or take a few years", when Benjamin Norman first settled at the site in 1883, See; Ben Norman's account.

Taking all things into consideration; we challenge the notion that the James "Pea vine Jimmy" Walton's threshing barn, allegedly recognized as the 2nd oldest log bldg. in the County of Spokane, Nine Mile Falls Spokane House, may have been built for Benjamin Norman, for the purpose of drying grass hay for the Norman Ranch.

"Possessory claims." – A claim of one who has settled on and improved public lands with the declared intention of patenting title is a "possessory claim." The adverse possessor must claim exclusive possession of the land, making p*hysical* improvement of the land, either by the construction of fences or houses, and or running livestock and constructing buildings or other improvements). [18]

According to Hugh Burnett's account; he stated that the Threshing Barn was present in 1883 the same year that the Reverend Charles Compton Burnett's family settled on the land. They noted the presence of three old buildings: the Threshing Barn, a log cabin with a stone fireplace at the center, and another highly deteriorated log cabin that soon after was dismantled. Charles Burnett's son;
Hugh Burnett, later described the Threshing Barn as it appeared in 1883:

"About half a mile south of the mouth of the Little Spokane and toward the Spokane River there was then standing a log building built of peeled logs.  The roof timbers were fastened on with wooden pegs and the roof, of cedar shakes, was also fastened on with wooden pegs. The building was built up with a log enclosure at each end and a threshing floor in the middle. At that time it had a floor made of logs hewn by hand.  On this floor the Indians threshed their grain, either by using a flail or by putting in two or three Cayuse ponies to trample the grain out" (Lewis 1925).

**On the other hand, Burnett's account of ponies trampling grain,** contradicts Daniel Drumheller's account Feb. 9th 1916; D. M. Drumheller described it like this;

"An old over-shot water mill was situated at Selheim springs just upriver from the little Spokane Rivers mouth, at the site of the Old Spokane House, when he first saw the point of land as it appeared at the junction of the Spokane and Little Spokane Rivers, during his travels through the HBC site in 1880, when he said nobody was there, at Selheim Springs, a few miles above the mouth of the little Spokane River, there was an old over-shot wooden water wheel, which he thought was used by the Hudson's Bay people for a saw mill or for grinding grain."

Daniel Drumheller's account deserves a mention as a *secondary-source* of information.  He mentioned the old dilapidated buildings w/ chimneys being there.

Curiously enough, Mr. Drumheller's contributions never mention *the builder, "Pea vine Jimmy"?*

*A repeated pattern* of accounts may be interpreted as a way to *circumvent the builder.*

**Taking everything into account**; we question as to why the Natives would need to "use a flail" or "trample grain w/ ponies" as Hugh Burnett implied, if a mill was in close proximity?

Aubrey L. White now "Montvale Farm" and Jay P. Graves "Waikiki Ranch" were partners in mining, they later formed the Miner-Graves Syndicate in 1896. Mr. Graves of "Waikiki ranch" was formerly known as Chief Garry's "In-chi-ten-see" and then later Adolph Selheim owner of "Selheim Springs," was then followed by Thomas Griffith of "Glen Tana Farms," and then followed by Mr. J. P. Graves "Gordon's fish hatchery". [19]

Chapter 7
## The Old Mill – "Selheim Springs"

A very old over-shot water mill photo taken by Binkley & White 1898
"Views of Montvale" - photo courtesy (Weaver family)

The origin of the mill in the photo is still unknown, however the mill's dilapidated appearance in the 1898 black and white picture taken by John Binkley and Aubrey White looks old enough to be (Yantis-1850's-Garry's mill) that was once located on the very spot of Selheim springs – presently known as the Spokane Fish (WDFW) hatcheries. "Views of Montvale" hand written by Binkley", are from a collection of letter's and photos, from a (descendant of Binkley/White). At present, the Weaver's are the owners of "Montvale Farm".

Lawrence Kip (1837-1899) was an officer who served w/ Colonel George Wright's (1803-1865) 1858 ruthless campaign to punish the opposition – which in this case was the Native American Indians for their Steptoe defeat of Colonel Edward Steptoe (1816-1865) the previous spring. As soldiers swept through Spokane Valley, Kip reported "coming across four Indian lodges, filled with wheat, which we burned."

**The story goes**; that in 1858 during Colonel Wright's campaign many Native tribes in the Spokane territory were harvesting and threshing grain along the Spokane River. In the early years these Indian houses were filled with grain, and later were destroyed at Colonel Wright's command, "excepting the Spokane Indian village where the mouth opens on the Little Spokane" where the Natives were busy growing a large quantity of grain in the region. Allegedly, where Judge Benjamin Yantis along with Chief Garry, a Spokan Native from the "Children of the Sun tribe" was operating a flour mill in 1859 located just upriver from "Birchwood Farm" at "Selheim Springs." The action of Colonel Wright paradoxically appears different in regard to the Selhiem mill left standing, undisturbed, while under his command, because of "Yantis/Invincibles", during the time of Native American-Warfare when the military was busy burning Native lodges, filled with wheat in the 1850's? [20]

We suggest; that the small gristmill was built c. (1859-1898), and after 30 years of abandonment fell into a dilapidated condition. See 1898 photo. By Indian Dept. arrangement they may have removed the mill stones to the little Pend Oreille River known today as the Oppenheimer Mill. Worth a read; The Old Dominion Mine of Colville with Secretary Simon Oppenheimer from the 1891 Financial and Mining Record, Vol.

30. And the other, Governor George *Simpson* (1787-1860) of *Rupert's Land* relative to the Hudson's Bay Company, London, March 1, 1829.

Our historical revisionism of the "two mill sites", and the "old building" located at Spokane House, may appear somewhat unconventional, if judged alongside the official version.   On the other hand a paradox may not be contradictory when examined more closely. We expect, our version of events will no doubt, enter into the mainstream of conflicting theories.  To help clear up any obscure assertions, throw into the mix a number of tantalizing truths.  If one opens the doors to their mind – that might be otherwise closed off to others opinions – their "preconceived ideas may or may not change" – opposite the conventional story.  Nonetheless, whether or not a re-interpretation of events, presented herein is imposed - is entirely up to the readers.
Only time will tell.

James Walton lived under an assumed name – a familiar known as "Pea vine Jimmy," who lived in Chattaroy.  Most of the early pioneers in the Wash. Terr. were either, Hudson's Bay Company employees, family members of the military, the United Brethren; missionaries to Native Americans, Quakers, and or Huguenots.  If a few of the early Chattaroy families *familiarly* knew and recognized James Walton simply as "*Pea vine Jimmy*" then they were supposed to know.  "*They*" may have even been familiar as to the meaning behind James Walton's pseudonym. Many of these early pioneers descend from generational newspaper families, and as such; are privy to insider information.  Not unlike, C. Compton Burnett who was the editor and publisher of the NEWS-DEMOCRAT in Spokane Falls - established in 1887. [21]

Even after James "Pea vine Jimmy" Walton's death, the enigma of the building is still puzzling.  The purpose for its use is left open to interpretation.  He may have built the said "building", but it was Ben Norman who built the first "meeting house" in 1884, aka the Clark house presently situated at "Birchwood."
B. Norman had cottages built by Kirtland K. Cutter on Adar Rd.  A question arose herein, and as such we've made inquires to the (park) as to the previous buildings?

Quakers, (Friends or Strangers) are members of a historically Christian group of religious movements aka as the Religious Society of Friends.

The historical societies share the same interest and agendas today; that is to record the accounts of past events, and that of the genealogy of its early pioneer's.

James Walton a descendent of a close-knit and multi-generational Quakers; makes clear that a building built at the site may have been built as a "meeting house" for Quakers in the territory of Washington. Mr. Walton and Mr. Cowgill were both Quakers and pioneer merchants in the close-knit community of Chattaroy. A similar scenario played out in Ohio, where Osborn Monnet and George Walton founded via the (Religious Society of Friends) the United Brethren (U. B.) Church, which was re-used later as the "Monnett School House" and then designated for animal quarters.

A vital clue **that has been overlooked by historians leaves an untold story;** In this we unveil James Walton, his Friends, and merchant partners. One such "well-to-do" partner was B. F. (Frank) Goodman. The two pioneers are listed on the Stevens County census record in the Colville, Wash. Terr. State Archives. In 1878 the territorial sheriff and enumerator, John U. Hofstetter *duly noted* James Walton's profession as a *miner*. An interesting tidbit is that John U. Hofstetter had a small piece of property in Mercer County, Ohio.

At a later date, the territorial sheriff and enumerator, G. B. Ide duly noted Frank Goodman as a farmer. In 1882, James Walton removed to Kidd/Chattaroy.

Some historians have made the claim that the stagecoach traveled on through to Spokane House, on its way to Colville, 'at a time' when the Native tribes were still roaming free in the Washington Territory, with settlers few and far between.

We think it makes more sense, based on our newly uncovered evidence; that rode the stage coach from the Station-Keepers Deep Creek along the way to the Cottonwood Road on Dragoon Creek, where James

Walton managed a livery stable-General Store, with the help of his close "Friends," Frank and Gilbert. In 1883 two merchant partners, James' and Frank' met with the territorial sheriff, G. B. Ide at the "Walton & Goodman store" once located upriver from the HBC on the Cottonwood Road, at the mouth of Dragon Creek and the little Spokane River. Gilbert Ide, 'at the time' was the territorial sheriff from 1886-1890 of Stevens, Pend Oriellle, Ferry and Okanogan counties. Mr. Ide was the son in-law of Mr. Jacob Stitzel. Gilbert Ide's intention was to build a light stage line for handling the mail to accommodate a number of small post offices en route. Mr. Ide, the first postmaster in Meyers Falls, established the Post Office there in 1891 running concurrently with that of James Walton's forage station sited where the mouth opens at Dragoon Creek.

**The Washington Territory Census and the Bureau of Land Mgmt. docs;** confirm that Mr. Walton did indeed homestead one hundred sixty acres at Dragoon. Additionally Frank Goodman was busy operating a store to be found at Fort Colville, Stevens County, where he first arrived to the territory in 1873 to Old Fort Colville. [22]

**At some point; we came across John Kidd a pioneer lawyer appt. the first-** prothonotary of Lycoming Pennsylvania in 1795. Ellis **Walton**, another lawyer, of Muncy was later appt. as the second recorder/clerk in 1809. Ellis Walton (1771-1813) was raised on his father's farm at the mouth of Glade Run, Muncy. James "Pea vine Jimmy" Walton is related to Ellis Walton.
The "Muncy Farms" plantation later became known as the "Halls Farms."

**Other parallels between Walton and Kidd/ Chattaroy connections;**
Could the Kidd/ Chattaroy, W.T. Post Office have been named after John Kidd? John Kidd was the secretary of the oldest secret society/ Masonic lodge 'at the time' in Lycoming County, Penn, where an angry mob of anti-masons tried to stop the first meeting in 1829. Rev. Henry Lenhart was the secretary. [23]

Robert P. Cowgill opened a general merchandise store in the same territory – about the same time as 'Walton & Goodman.' Mr. Cowgill carried the mail from Spokane to Chattaroy, Kidd P.O., and engaged in mining and farming. Fraternally Robert Cowgill was a charter member of some early Masonic Lodges in Chattaroy. He later married Margaret M. Lang, in 1879. Mr. and Mrs. Cowgill were *Quakers*.

Chapter 8
## MINING DISCOVERIES - COPPER, SILVER & GOLD

Valuable mineral deposits had been discovered in California – 1840's-50's; Nevada and Colorado - 1850s; Idaho and Montana - 1860s; South Dakota and the Black Hills – the mid-1870s. James Walton and Frank Goodman were amongst early prospectors and miners in Deadwood, South Dakota. Goodman made a fortune in the Black Hills, Dakota Territory, a sacred place of broken treaties and broken hearts. A result of diminished lands of the Lakota Nation aka Great Sioux, Native American's when gold was discovered in the Black Hills. B. F. Goodman was robbed by bandits for $25,000 during a stage coach ride through the Deadwood, Canyon Springs.

In the early 1880's the widespread mining excitement would not have gone unnoticed by master metallurgists such as, the Norman bros, "Ben and Billy" and their partner, a well-known Pacific Northwest "MINING KING" James Breen. Surely 'they got wind of the Old Dominion mine' early on. They were likely acquainted with James Walton and his mining and merchant partner Frank Goodman, either directly or indirectly. This 'begs the question," why Ben Norman, curiously enough did not make mention of James "Pea vine Jimmy" Walton in his own account. Interestingly enough, after reading the accounts of Benjamin Norman, Daniel Drumheller, and the Burnett bros. among others, neither of them acknowledges James "Pea vine Jimmy" Walton, (a secret pioneer who lived in a secret world apart from 'outsiders' for a very long time). But with almost certainty "they" knew about him.

James Walton's life-story follows along a similar vine as that of B. Norman – given that he lived in the Washington Territory simultaneously nearby the Hudson's Bay Company. If Mr. Walton's origin has indeed

been kept a secret, "the question remains, why then?" Perhaps they were attempting to *veil* his true identity of (Quaker roots, and or French Huguenot descent) – masking a Royal bloodline coursing through his veins? His origin has remained elusive for some time now.
James Walton does indeed have some very interesting relatives and ancestors.

Benjamin Norman arrived to the W. T. (Wash) in 1882 - marking a momentous year for the *first* mineral discovery east of Colville, Stevens County district - setting the stage for active work in the Old Dominion mine in 1885. Assays of their mineral deposits taken to Spokane were good enough, that they returned and located several more claims. It was, B. F. Goodman who discovered the Ella claim on Dominion Mountain, where he owned a ten acre homestead nearby. Goodman was still the superintendent of the Old Dominion mine, the same year that James Walton passed away on December 5th 1907. Benjamin Norman was a capitalist, intimately connected with the Spokane Stock Exchange. He would have been privy to 'insider' knowledge early on, relatively speaking of the Old Dominion. [24]

The highly respected Rev. Jonathan Edwards implied that Mr. Walton had invested five hundred twenty five dollars for a twenty first interest in the American Mining Company on July 7th 1850. Based on new evidence herein; the mining Company was operating twenty years before incorporating in 1911, - representing the interest of Albert and Reinhold Kleinschmidt. On a side note; might Albert and Reinhold Kleinschmidt be related to Brother John C. Kleinschmidt (United Brethren) of Pennsylvania, Ohio)? [25]

The name, James Walton appears on the Spokane County Washington Terr., Census - enumeration date; May 12, 1887, aged 57 years - a farmer, born in 1830 Pennsylvania New York. (We contradict this info; and suggest he was born in Ohio.)

Frank Goodman (1837-1922), Gilbert B. Ide and John U. Hofstetter were among the charter members who started the Stevens County Pioneer association - beginning on Oct. 1st 1903, in which Jacob Stitzel was the first president, and in 1914 B. F. Goodman was the pres.

Membership was restricted to residents of the state prior to June, 1895. (In all likelihood, this would be the first families of Virginia (ffv).

Frank Goodman passed away while in the Keller Store on Dec. 11, 1922. The Stevens County Pioneer association performed funeral services. William C. Keller and G. B. Ide, were among the pallbearers, and Mrs. Keller performed the music.

"Pea vine Jimmy" was known to an initiated obscure group cut off from "outsiders". So the general population was unaware of his identity. But, the Stevens County Pioneer historical society recognized *James Walton* intimately. They make mention of him using his (mining initiation nickname Pea vine Jimmy) in Frank Goodman's obituary/eulogy within a 1922 Colville examiner newspaper. [26]

## Chapter 9
### "PEA *VINE* JIMMY" - Origin Unknown - *A Eureka Moment*;

With respect to our research, we experienced an epiphany, when we cite a bible verse; "Keep asking and it will be given to you. Keep searching, and you will find. Keep knocking, and the door will be opened to you.

Matthew 7:7, Seek, and ye shall find: "James was born on Dec 5th 1830, son of David Walton (1796-1853), and Louisa Winchell (1807-1875)." His BIRTH originated just five years after his parents arrival into the Ohio terr., by way of horse and wagon teams in 1825. The Walton's were Pennsylvania German pioneers. The Walton family traveled to Ohio in horse and wagon teams accompanied by family, akin to Thomas and Martha Johnston. The Johnston's had numerous children, one of which was Henry Drinker Ellis Johnston, a prominent freemason. Walton, Monet, Johnston, Warner, and Wright pioneer families were circuit riding traveling itinerant preachers of generational Quakers/Friends. By way of wagon train, these families may have traveled alongside the United Brethren missionaries on their way to Ohio. In 1889, a disagreement arose over membership in *secret societies*, the *Freemasons,* the *church's constitution*, and other issues split the **U. B.** into majority liberal and minority conservative blocs, the latter, was led by Bishop Milton *Wright* –the (father of the *Wright* Brothers).

James Walton grew up on the Walton family farm in Crawford County Ohio. In 1850 leaving home for the first time on his 20th birthday, he embarks for the California gold rush, only to return three years later.

Embedded within Edwards's book; (A History of Spokane 1900); are a few vital clues that may have been overlooked by historians. What is read between the lines is the reason why James went back to Ohio in the first place.

"Clues' that turn into facts; those prove indispensable." Edwards seemed to know *key details* about James Walton aka "Pea vine Jimmy" whilst at the same time he remained an enigma to him. He was unsure as to the reason why James Walton returned home in 1853, and whether or not the state was Ohio or Indiana? 'Case in point' the author's herein has since learned the reason why James returned home. It was to pay his respects; in honor of the passing of his father, and one brother.

*Our* narratives are uniquely unconventional opposite the official narratives of James Walton to date. We tell the story from different points of view. We agree to disagree with opposing views as a form of our "Freedom of Speech & Expression."

**According to the National Archives document;** there is a very real possibility that James' along with his *Friend* and partner, B. F. Goodman, traveled side by side, during their journey on the ship sailing to California by way of Isthmus Panama, to seek their fortunes in the California gold rush.

The names; B. F. Goodman and J. Walton are listed on the San Francisco Ship roster (1851-1852). With James Walton's eulogy/ obituary details James Walton's details of his journey, as well. *In particular*, that James had twice walked from his hometown in Marion Ohio to the gold fields and the mining camps in California. We have tried to separate the previous notions of sensationalism; *deciphering fact from fiction*. The probability that James Walton did indeed travel by ship vs. walking can be eliminated from the *author's herein consideration*. Based on even more facts from Ohio the 2,400-mile trip on average could have taken *James Walton and Frank Goodman* anywhere from four or five months to arrive safely to San Francisco (if he or they) did indeed really walk the entire journey? Even if they had traveled with the **U. B. Brethren** by wagon trains, they risked exposure to the weather, wagons breaking down, Native American attacks, sickness, disease, bandits, and so on. Worse-case scenario, if these two had waited to long, they would have missed out on mining claims. They most likely traveled by stagecoach on their way to California. [27]

Following ten years as a gold seeker, prospector and placer miner James' returns home. After shaking off the fever, he again leaves making the long journey back to California. He traveled quite extensively as 'a man of means,' and was well connected with '*Friends*' and distinct mining magnates with power and influence.

In 1873 Frank Goodman accompanied Jacob Stitzel, (Washington State land commissioner) to the Colville Territory, and it is entirely possible that James Walton may have traveled alongside them, with the "Father of Spokane" James Glover when he arrived to Spokane. Mr. Goodman and Mr. Stitzel began the Stevens County Pioneer Association in Colville on Oct. 1, 1903, and also played a part on the committee of the constitution and by-laws, in which Mr. Stitzel was president.

**Walton – Monnett;** Noble blood runs through the family *veins*, via the intermarriage of James Walton's, brother in-law, Augustus Eddy Monnett (1845–1917), who wedded Dorothy Annie Walton (1849-1905), on February 25th 1868. The Monnett family lineage is well-documented elsewhere in the interest of genealogy. Abraham Edward Monnet's lineal descent is traced direct from the French Noble Vines of the Huguenots. The Monnet's originated in France and migrated to America early on - 1700's. The Monet/Money family descends from French Kings and British Royalty. Imagine for a moment, that the "Pea vine Jimmy" building that is a landmark may have been built by a Frenchman - with ancient bloodlines running through his veins. James Walton's background origin reveals more than the simple beginnings of a humble-old log building; hence the "Pea vine Jimmy" legacy. He invested heavily in mining, and was a "key "partner in the midst of 'pioneer power players.'

James Walton was allied to Monet (Monnett/*Money*/Moneta), via his sister's marriage. One mining and moneyman acted out herein is Mervin J. Monnett.

Allegorically speaking, on a closer inspection one learns that Juno Moneta is an epithet of Juno a "protector" of funds. The irony here is that in 1907 Mervin Monnett protected his gold with armed guards located at Mohawk mine in Tonapah, Nevada.

James Walton's family tree is to numerous to list here, and as such a brief genealogical, historical and biographical sketch for history sake may suffice. His ancestry is documented by Birchwood Farm Grove; Find a Grave Memorial ID 184294951). Our primary concern traces the intermarriage between Walton, Monet/Monnette, Jonson/Johnston, Chastain and the Hall families-Hall Farms aka "Muncy Farms".

Most of these allied families are prominent founding members and Freemasons in Marion, Bucyrus, and Crawford County Ohio - title holders to large tracts of land. In 1864 Abraham Monnet organized the Marion Farmers bank in which he was the President. Abraham's sons/son in laws was the initial *stock-keepers* of the bank. The Bank of America in Los Angeles was established in 1923 by <u>Orra E. Monnette</u>. In 1928, *Giannini* became a close business associate with the bank pres. Monnette. The Monnett Chapel is a historic church at 999 OH 98 in Bucyrus, Ohio. The Methodist Episcopal Church aka "M. E. Church has been added to the Historic National Register.

Abraham Monnett was a granger, fraternally connected with the Ohio Grange in the late-1880's, actively engaged in farming, stock-dealing, mining and banking. The Monnett's descend from Huguenot families who escaped Henry the 1V in the Edict of Nantes - from ancient nobility given to France in the Province of Bearn. Henry of Navarre-king of France from (1589-1610) was the leader of the Huguenot armies 'at a time' when he succeeded the Catholic Henry the 3rd a founder of the Bourbon dynasty in 1589 thereby establishing religious freedom in France. [28]

**One of many Monnett descendents of recognition Frank Sylvester; aka** Francis S. Monnett (1857) was an Ohio Attorney-general from (1896-1900). He beat an important case that led to the permanent break-up of the Standard Oil Trust, established by John D. Rockefeller.

Sadly out of the blue, Frank's wife was accidentally shot by a boy hunting "rats and or rabbits". Mrs. Monnett did manage to recover from her injuries. [29]

Henry Johnson later married Jane Ludwig, b. 11-20-1831, the daughter of Samuel Ludwig, a native of Berks, County, Pennsylvania, originally from Alsace, France. The Ludwig brothers were from France, "devoted Huguenots". Mr. Frank Alexander Stivers married Zua Johnston of Bucyrus, Ohio, the daughter of Henry and Jane Ludwig Johnston Monnett. Their second son Richard Johnston was born in 1893 at Ripley, Ohio. Later on he became a student at Yale University, New Haven, Connecticut the mysterious "Skull & Bones" Society, known informally as "Bones".
The Rev. Jonathan Edwards (1703-1758), entered Yale College in 1716

The Russell Trust Association owns the society's real estate. Only fifteen members/ bonesmen are inducted in any one year in the society. Thomas J. Monnett married Henrietta Johnston on 10-17-1847 the daughter of Thomas F. and Martha (Walton) Johnston, wealthy and highly respected pioneers of Marion County, Ohio. [30]

One of James Walton's aunts' Martha (1803-1881) married Thomas F. Johnston (1800-1862) on September 20, 1823. Martha L. (Walton) Johnston was the daughter of David and Elizabeth (Rogers) Walton, born in Lycoming, County Pennsylvania. Her grandfather Walton was one of three brothers who came to America, from England. *On a side note*, could Martha Walton be a descendant from one of the four Byberry Waltons? Byberry Philadelphia County, Pennsylvania, was settled by Swedes before 1675, during which that same year four brothers—Nathaniel, Thomas, Daniel and William **Walton** arrived at Newcastle from England. The brothers prospected the land nearby the *banks* of the Delaware River, Poquessing Creek settling down in caves, as did the Swedes before them, and were early members of the Society of *Friends* (Quakers). (The early Essenes also settled in caves.) [31]

## Chapter 10
## *Birchwood Farm*

William Stanley Lewis was the Corresponding Secretary of the Spokane Historical Society. The objective was to collect and record a large collection of manuscript. Their similar dialogue of immortalized stories, after their death becomes the property of others, a-man-u-en-sis, re-told time and time again. It is interesting to note; by their own accounts, that neither Benjamin Norman nor the Burnett brothers ever mention - "Pea vine Jimmy" - when referencing the buildings built at Spokane House. Ben's details of the building/ buildings vary little with Hugh Burnett's. Neither Ben nor the Burnett brothers deviate from their own detailed accounts – in which case, W. S. Lewis reveals in 1925; Few men among the early settlers of the Spokane country had a better appreciation or the value of or greater interest in the early history of this region, than Ben Norman owner of the Spokane Hotel. For his careful observation and retentive memory we are indebted for many interesting details concerning the early history of the Spokane region. Mr. Norman's statement as transcribed verbatim from my notes: [32]

The photo below was taken by the Spokesman Review in the early-1880s, a courtesy of the Northwest Room Downtown Spokane Library. We're not entirely sure where the mansion sat. The Lewis and Clark High School at present situates on or nearby the grounds of Ben Normans home once situated on 5th and Stevens. Ben's address on 5th is documented by Spokane Polk's phone/ address book

"BENJAMIN NORMAN RESIDENCE"
Spokesman Review circa 1880's

**In May, 1882, I left England**

The death of my mother had broken my chief home tie and I was restless. I had friends in many parts of the world and sufficient money for my needs, so I sailed for America. I had an Irish friend named Adams. He had gone out to the Heppner, Oregon country some years before, invested in sheep and accumulated a small fortune. This he had taken to Boston and, investing it in the grain business, and lost it all. He proposed that I go into the sheep business with him. I consented and he met me in New York on my arrival and we came out west together. We left the train at the end of steel on the Northern Pacific, a little station named Bedford, in eastern Montana. From there we took a stage coach into Helena. There we engaged a mule team and drove over the mountains to Herron, or some neighboring station, which was then the western end of construction on the road.  Bishop Tuttle, the pioneer bishop of Montana, accompanied us on the trip.

**Visited Spokane Falls**; While Adams took our stuff to Missoula and arranged for an outfit, I came on through to the coast.  On my way, I stopped off for a few days at the settlement of Spokane Falls.  I returned to Montana and meeting my friend Adams at Missoula, we took a buckboard and camping outfit going over the Blackfoot trail into the northern part of Montana; we traveled about and camped out all summer looking for a favorable location for our sheep ranch.  We returned to Helena in the fall still undecided and selling our outfit, my friend Adams returned to the east while I came back to Spokane Falls.  The town had a population of some 500 people.  It was an attractive little place.  I liked the climate and I had become acquainted with some nice people so I decided to remain here.

**Favorite Camping Ground**; In 1883 I acquired land in the vicinity of the mouth of the Little Spokane River on the peninsula between the big and the Little Spokane Rivers.  Though the Spokane Indian reservation had been established a short time before, the place was still a favorable camping ground of Indians of different tribes.  Old Indians have told me that the place had always been a favorite meeting place for catching and curing fish and for trade and barter by members of the different western tribes.  In those early days, the black soil of the lower bench land lying along the two rivers was scored deeply with the numerous trails, evidently worn by the travel of many generations of wandering Indians and their ponies.  Up the bluff and leading to the second bench, there are still evidences of the main trail showing signs of heavy labor.

**Preparing Private Cache**; This word "cache" was a common term among early pioneers and Indians.  A hole was dug in a suitable dry place, lined with bark, grass and sticks and property one wanted to leave behind was carefully stored away in the hole which was then covered with cloth, hide or bark and filled up with dirt.  The hole was then tramped over, and the dirt packed and leveled, and the surplus dirt thrown away so as to leave no trace to show the existence of the cache.  Hidden property was often left for months or even several years.  From time to time I explored some of these old caches but found nothing of interest. Another fact going to prove the peaceful history of this neighborhood is that while the plow has turned up many stone pestles and mortars used for crushing the camas root into flour I know of few arrows or spear heads ever found there. Stone mortars are occasionally turned up by the plow on both sides of the river and are found even more plentifully two miles up the little Spokane near Struman's bridge.

**Pick up Indian relics;** John Binkley, whose farm is near the bridge, has an interesting collection of Indian relics found near his place. They are of considerable interest. Arrow heads, stone war hammers, as well as a number of skulls and some human bones, have been picked up there. Chief Joseph, I believe, visited the vicinity in early days and spoke of the Indian tradition of a great Indian fight there between different tribes in the dim past. Chief Joseph could give no explanation of the hieroglyphics or painted rocks.

Painted rocks – picture taken by Binkley
Photo courtesy – "Montvale Farms"

"Anthromorphic, geomorphic & zoomorphic, painted rocks; - depict the sun, lizards, animal images and buffalo, while other pictographs are indecipherable."

.

Chief Garry of the (Middle) Spokane Indians with whom I have often talked was no better informed as to the origin or meaning of those painted rocks.

The Indians had evidently had originally used the whole of the valley, more or less, at the junction of the two rivers, but the salmon drying frames of most of the tepees were on the south side of the river in the vicinity of the fish traps on the little Spokane river. The stone remains of those fish traps may still be traced.

**Spokane Garry Had Facts;** Most of my information about the place was obtained from Old Spokane Garry.

Garry when but a small boy, had been sent across the mountains by the officers of the Hudson's Bay Company to be educated at St. Boniface. He was a most intelligent Indian and he could converse fluently in both English and French. The land I settled on was railroad land and the summer I bought it, I camped out on the lace. Chief Garry used to ride through my place often. He was fond of tea and I often used to make it for him. He told me that the spot had always been a great meeting for the Indians. The different tribes used to assemble there before they went across the mountains for the buffalo hunt. They used to collect in large numbers so as to be able to go in sufficient force to resist their enemies, the Blackfeet and the Crows. These parties usually joined the Kootenai and the Flatheads before crossing the mountains.

**Great Fishing Place;** The place was also a great fishing place. The Indians had fish traps across both the main Spokane River and the Little Spokane River, and there were fish for everyone. When I first settled there the fish were so plentiful it was almost no sport to catch them. The fish would reach the spawning grounds at the headwaters of the stream. John Stevens was settled on part of my land, but the Indian agent compelled him to move to the Indian reservation. The (middle) Spokane Indians were salmon people. I had read Washington Irving's "Astoria," and I was greatly interested in this point of land where I settled as being that described by Irving as the site of the Spokane trading post of Astor's Pacific Fur Company. When Mr. Burnett settled on the site in 1883 there were several buildings standing on the site of various ages.

**Indians Erected Mounds;** How much truth there was in these stories about the stone heaps; I, of course, can not say. About six miles southwest of this point were several of the principal old Indian trails converged on the plain alongside of a large basaltic boulder, four similar Indian mounds of cairns (a heap of stones as a monument or landmark) of stone erected by Indians on the top of the boulder have given the name four Mound Prairie to the region where the boulder stands.

It was evident to me that the neck of land at the junction of the two rivers was a much used trading post and a peaceful meeting place of many tribes. On the higher ground on both sides of the river, there are still to be seen some evidences of many old caches (a hiding place for food and supplies for future use, used by explorers; anything hidden in such a place.) Many are in close proximity to each other, showing that these wandering tribes felt safe in leaving their worldly possessions behind them.

**Ben Recalls Old Buildings;** About half a mile south of the mouth of the Little Spokane and toward the main Spokane River there was an old threshing barn built of peeled logs. Some 200 yards east of this and near the Little Spokane River, there was a two-room log cabin of peeled cedar logs with a stone fireplace in the center between the two rooms.

Berg's pic 2009

Riverside State Park - "Pea vine Jimmy"
Old building still standing near the boat launch

Both buildings were roofed with cedar shakes and probably 25 years old. I was informed that the two-room cabin had been used as a road house or stopping place on the Colville trail or road which crossed the little Spokane at a ford near the mouth of the stream. North of these two buildings and near the slough, there was a third log building badly decayed and apparently much older than the other buildings. This might have been part of the employees' quarters of the old trading post. A quarter of a mile or so south of the buildings first described, there was an old cemetery covering about an acre. Many of the graves were sunken. It had the appearance of an old cemetery. There were probably 100 of these enclosed graves.

**Old Chimney Bottoms;** South and west from this burying place toward the south bank of the Spokane River and about half a mile south of the building first described, there were some old foundations and remains of chimney bottoms that could clearly be traced in 1883. There were also some large holes in parallel lines which probably indicated the existence of former cellars, though they might have been pits for baking camas. They were rather large for camas pits.

This was probably the actual site of the old trading posts of 1812. In clearing up the land, Mr. Burnett tore down the grave enclosures, rolled the loose boulders into the cellar holes and cultivated the land. This was owned by B. L. Gordon and partly occupied by an orchard. For some time, a stage ran from Glover's stable at Spokane Falls through this point of land to Chewelah and Colville. The route was also used for a time to reach Fort Spokane. Going to Fort Spokane, one continued along the north side of the Spokane River to La Pray's bridge and then crossed to the south side and continued west to the fort.

**Trail to Spokane;** On the upper flat or bench, this trail branches in two, one following east up the little Spokane river and connecting with old Kalispell trail, running east and north, and the other running along the west side of Five Mile Prairie to the old fork in the Spokane river somewhere below the present Spokane public library. I might mention as an interesting fact that where this old trail reached the second bench on the Little Spokane, there is still in existence the conical heap of stones which old Indians have told me was used in early days as a sort of post office by traveling Indians, who by placing certain rocks in which they picked to convey information to their friends behind as to the direction taken. – By Benjamin Norman
On another note it is Worth a read- W. S. Lewis; The Case of Chief Garry

**(On the 16th day of Oct. 1885 the Rev. Compton C. Burnett filed for a** homestead where the two rivers meet; at the Receiver's land Office from J. M. Adams (register) for N.P.R.R. railroad land. The homestead claim required homesteaders to farm and make improvements for 5 years before "proving up" eligibility).

At a time when the Burnett family was busy *"proving up"* on their homestead; the said land was in all likelihood tied up in the Supreme Court in Washington State & Washington D. C., until April 12th 1890 by Enoch a Spokan Native, who was previously promised other Railroad land on the mouth of the Spokane & little Spokane River. As a result of Enoch being once located on the land Downtown Spokane, known as the "Shanty-town Case," 'all the while' other Natives, such as; John, Simon and Jeremiah all lost land in the same area. John Stevens, a Native who had initially settled on Benjamin Normans land, which touched along side a common boundary adjacent to the Burnett's homestead.

Berg's photo
Sarah & Rev. C. Compton Burnett & family
Greenwood Cemetery Spokane, Washington

The Rev. Charles C. Burnett passed away in 1887. Four years later the homestead proof was approved on July 3rd 1891. In all probability, Sarah, a widowed mother was finally able to purchase the home-stead legally on record, because Enoch had lost the said land in the Supreme Court Shanty-town case. The N.P.R.R. surveyed the land in 1885, interestingly at about the same time that B. F. Goodman (engineer/surveyor) was in the W. T. with his Friend James (Pea vine Jimmy) Walton.

Almost five years later, on April 6th 1890, Sarah Burnett, a widowed mother was able to prove up on the homestead.

"Possessory claims." – A claim of one who has settled on and improved public lands with the declared intention of patenting title is a "possessory claim". The adverse possessor must claim exclusive possession of the land, making p*hysical* improvement of the land, either by the construction of fences or houses, and or running livestock and constructing buildings or other improvements). [33]

H. L. Moody arrived to Spokane in the Washington territory in 1886, where he established the "Moody Land Company." His Spokane residence was designed by Arthur W. Cowley, an architect/craftsman whose father Henry Thomas Cowley originated with the first families (FFV) in the territory of Washington. Mr. Cowley owned and edited the Spokane Chronicle between the years (1883-87), Cowley's name translates the (son of Olaf), an old Manx family. Rev. Cowley was a missionary to the Nez Perce, the Spokane's and other tribal affiliations, who became personally involved with Chief Enoch in the Spokane Shantytown-War. [34]

Charles and Sarah Burnett are both listed on the BLM record as purchasing 150 ac. of property nearby the Vets hospital in Spokane on April 1st 1890. It is likely that his wife Sarah included his name on the purchase because her husband was deceased during the time of record recorded between April 1st 1890-April 30th 92. [35]

The Rev. Charles Compton Burnett was born in Hampshire England (1835-1887) his wife was Sarah Ann Burnett (1837-1920) Trafford. In 1884 the Rev. C. C. Burnett was the first resident rector of the All Saints, Episcopal Church located in Spokane Falls, Washington Territory. The Trafford family connected to the Astor family, through business deals between Edward R. Trafford's land conveyances in Florida between William Backhouse Astor. In 1884 the Trafford Sanford C. E. map of the Sanford land grant donated lands for sale by Edward R. Trafford, by the Florida Land Colonization Co. [36]

Mr. Norman, Mr. and Mrs. Burnett, James Walton, and Frank Goodman were in the same Washington territory intertwining at that time with the "Shanty-town" Supreme Court case via Chief Enoch (who was initially *Promised Land* here by the Railroad (160 acres) in trade for his "downtown Spokane land" taken from him). [37]

Imagine that Ben, a Nine Mile resident, may have affectionately named "Birchwood Farm" after "Birch Farm" a farm house from his youth located in his home town of Cheltenham, Clarence - Square. Ben's father George Norman noted; "Birch Farm" in his book – (Norman's Pictorial Hand-Book of Cheltenham in 1854).

The "Norman family Farm" spans four generations of lineal descendants of the CENTURY FARM NORMAN RANCH EST. 1883, that Ben later Incorporated in 1914. At the time of this writing; four acres and the original farmhouse remain with the Norman family. The rest of Birchwood aka Norman ranch is presently owned and managed by the Washington State Parks and Recreation Commission, (WSPRC). While closed off to 'outsiders' a majority of observers are outwardly oblivious to the old BFC, while on the other hand are well-informed of the better-known HBC. The author's herein; are allowing a free flow of information, and had previously unleashed in 1989 "context clues" in manuscript form - and here in published form-2017.

## Chapter 11
### ARTICLES OF INCORPORATION OF THE BIRCHWOOD FARM CO;

KNOW ALL MEN BY THESE PRESENTS, that we, Ben Norman of Tacoma, Pierce County and T. B. Higgins and R.E.M. Strickland of the City and County of Spokane, all of the State of Washington, citizens of the United States of America, have this day voluntarily associated ourselves together, for the purpose of forming a corporation under the laws of the state of Washington, authorizing the formation of private corporations; and we do hereby make, adopt and certify the following articles of incorporation:
ARTICLE 1.The name of this corporation shall be BIRCHWOOD FARM CO.
ARTICLE 11.The objects for which this corporation is formed are:

1. To acquire, hold, purchase, sell, convey, dispose of, rent and lease real and personal property of any and every kind whatsoever in the United States of America.
2. To locate, take, acquire, hold, purchase, bond, lease, sell, develop and *operate water rights* of any and every character flumes, and ditches, and to

construct and build the same for all the purposes and requirements of irrigating land; and *for the purpose of developing power and electricity for any and all purposes* in the United States of America.

Photo Courtesy "Kathleen Beard & her sister's Harriet & Mary Lou," Granddaughters of William & Amy Norman

A waterwheel once situated close-by Ben's original farmhouse at "Birchwood" nearby the Little Spokane River. L. B. Ness was the foreman for the Norman Ranch, where he found a "two foot fresh water eel" in the Reservoir, which was thrown up by the waterwheel that was once used between the 1880s-1890s at "Birchwood" for raising water for irrigation from the little Spokane River. The water *eel* was later displayed in a large fish tank in the Hotel Spokane.

3. To carry on a general farming business, and to engage in the business of stock-raising, dairying and fruit-growing.

In 1889 Sidney Norman wrote a letter to one of his son's Frank Winston Norman (1918-2006) about the fact, that "Uncle Ben was using a milking machine on the Norman Ranch in 1889." After reading the letter, we were taken aback; Ben had been privileged with the advantage of electrical power early on at 'Birchwood.' Ben's brother, William had numerous electrical patents, and was a close associate of electrical pioneer engineers; like; Sidney Mitchell and Fred Sparling, both agents of Thomas Edison Electric Illuminating Company; the main players of the water power. The powerhouse is located at the lower falls, one of the greatest water power stations in the war of the currents. In 1885 a few local capitalists built a small plant alongside the river running by one water wheel. It generated enough electricity for 12 arc lights and three hundred incandescent lights. In 1888 the Edison Electric Illuminating

Company of Spokane Falls absorbed the old company power plant. They then re-moved to the back of the C. & C. in the old post mill bldg.

Washington Water Power Company controlled the Edison Electric Illuminating Co, Spokane Street Railway Co, Spokane Electric and Ross Park St. Railway Co, and was the owners of the C. & C. flour mills, among the prominent officers were Ben Norman's brother, W. S. Norman; Treasurer, and F. Lewis Clark the 2nd V. P.
Mr. Clark mysteriously disappeared on a business trip. In 1884 Clark established the C. & O. Mill and Elevator, the largest flouring mill in the Pacific Northwest. [38]

In 1913 the W. W. P. recognized a milk house at the Norman Ranch for dairying, Nine Mile Falls, location. The Little Spokane River near mouth - water (s) Station #12431900 - the Geological water supply. These stations located along the Little Spokane River through Elk and Dartford was recorded (1911-1913) for the Water Resources data for Wash, Surface water supply. [39]

"Frank Julian Sprague (1857-1934), an inventor, scientist, and Engineer", aka "Father of Electric Traction." Frank J. Sprague became an agent for the Edison Co. and began his own company in 1884. In the early years, when an Edison installation required a motor, Sprague's Co. supplied it. He was the inventor of vertical and horizontal transportation. [40]

Berg's pic.                    Spokesman Review    Jan. 26, 1947

An electrical mini-hydro plant once located here. A boxed in electric switch supersedes a "water-wheel' in which the early settlers installed". The mill was used for dairying and farming. (Photo 1889 W. W. P. Co., W.S. Norman) [41]

"On the Little Spokane River, Nine Mile, The Mill/Lot 3, 12 mills were considered. The mini-hydro power plants could supply power for personal use - to a few tightly-knit neighboring farms - before the larger dams' construction that provided power to the larger communities - electrical power".

Washington Water Power Document

Little Spokane River Nine Mile, Mill/Lot 3

1889 C. N. Miller/Union Pacific Ry, Co.

4. To issue both preferred and common stock and to accept payment of subscriptions therefore in such installments, or in such matter, and in such property, real or personal, as shall be determined by a majority of the board of Trustees; to borrow money, issue bonds, notes, debentures, and other evidences of indebtedness; and to mortgage any all of its real or personal property; and to acquire; hold and dispose of options and stocks, bonds, notes and mortgages of other corporations and of individuals; and to acquire; hold and dispose of the bonds of this corporation; and to do every and all things convenient, proper or requisite for the carrying out of the objects and purposes in these articles, set forth in their fullest and broadest sense.

**ARTICLE 111.** The amount of the capital stock of this corporation shall be seventy five thousand (75,000) dollars, divided into seven hundred and fifty (750) shares of the par value of one hundred ($100.00) dollars each. "To put this into perspective; $75,000.00 in 1914 had the same buying power as $1,810,740.00 in 2017".

**ARTICLE 1V.** The principal place of business of this corporation shall be at Birchwood Farm, Nine Mile Falls in Spokane County, State of Washington; provided, however, that meetings of the trustees of said Corporation shall be held for the transaction of Corporation business in other places, upon due notice given as prescribed in the by-laws of the Company.

**ARTICLE V.** The term for which this Corporation shall exist is fifty (50) years.

Ben's Bungalow aka (BFC)            1914 BFC "stock certificate"

**ARTICLE V1.** The number of trustees in this Corporation shall be three who shall be elected by the stockholders of the Company; the number of trustees who shall manage the concerns of the Corporation until the first meeting, which shall be in less than six months, shall be three, and the names and residences of said trustees are as follows:

**1. Benjamin Norman (1846-1934) a resident of Tacoma, Wash;**
Ben the son of George and Honore Norman had a regal upbringing in Cheltenham Gloucester England, where he engaged as a wealthy coal merchant later on. He was rather nice looking, well dressed and groomed with a neatly trimmed mustache and beard, skillful in all wisdom, with good humor and of noble bloodline. In 1884, his brother William Shephard Norman a capitalist arrived in Spokane. The two brothers spent their schoolboy days among wealth and culture at the Cheltenham grammar School. Guided by High Level Freemasons, they were bestowed with ancient insider knowledge. The bros. early adult years were spent working within their father's newspaper business. The Norman brothers had an air about them –speaking of old world charm in the modern world. They had above average intellect, and were

multilingual in German, Latin and Ancient Greek. The two were coextensive amongst other widely known pioneer capitalists, mining magnates, railroad tycoons, and influential business men. They enjoyed good times for sure, in the midst of other Spokane millionaires. They were prominent amongst Spokane civic leader's and empire builder's early on in the Washington Territory. W. S. Norman was an avid Freemason, belonging to numerous club affiliations – with links to the Spokane Athletic Club, Arlington Club of Portland, the Rossland Club of Rossland, British Columbia, the Rocky Mountain Club of New York City and many more social fraternities, and club affiliations. Wm. Norman connected to members of the Spokane Club and the Spokane Country Club wherein; J. A. Finch was the first president. The Norman brothers were amongst the first pioneer charter members initiated into the Spokane Lodge, No. 228; B. P. O. E. Ben Norman was a charter member and the president in 1893-95 of the Spokane Club-Columbia Bldg, on the Lamona block adjoining the Spokane Hotel located on 1st Ave." [42]

**2. T. B. Higgins a resident of Spokane, Wash;** Thomas was born in Washington D.C., in 1859. Thomas became a lawyer in 1885 he removed to Spokane five years later. Mr. Higgins was a trustee for the Birchwood Farm Co., & the Northwestern and Pacific Hypotheek Bank farm mortgages. T. B. Higgins colleagues consisted of Frank Truman Post and Antoine Edward Russell. The three pioneer lawyers practiced in the Exchange National Bank Bldg, counseling for the W.W.P, Birchwood Farm Company, Pacific States Telephone & Telegraph Co., Home Tel & Tel Co., the Federal Mining And Smelting Co., the Holland-Washington Mtg., and various Insurance companies/corporations. The Post, Avery and Higgins law firm (1893-1900). A. G. Avery was a Spokane County Superior Court Judge, Spokane Corporation Counsel, U. S. District Attorney for Eastern Washington. A. G. Avery was pres. of the Spokane Club (1903-04). Mr. & Mrs. Evelyn Avery came to Spokane in 1888 and resided at 505 W. Rockwood Boulevard now recognized as the Avery-McClintock House. Frank T. Post was named president of the (W.W.P.C.) in 1930. Frank and his colleague, Antoine Russell were members of the Beta Theta Pi, Phi Beta Kappa Fraternities; original name "the Order of Skull and Bones," the Catalogue of Beta Theta Pi-Pg 840 / QEBH is a senior honor society at the University of Missouri. Russell founded in 1897 along with 6 others. [43]

3.  R. E. M. Strickland a resident of Spokane, Wash; Robert or aka "Bob" (1867-1933) was born in West Chester, Pennsylvania to Nimrod & Rosella (Gould) Strickland (1845-1922).  He's buried in his native state of West Chester, Pennsylvania in the Oakland Cemetery.  A question arose; are "Rosella (Gould) and Jason "Jay" Gould, robber baron (1836–1892) related?  In 1892-98 Robert Strickland later became a pioneer lawyer of Spokane and manager of the Sweeny investment Co., and the Pennsylvania Mtg. Co., located in Spokane's Columbia Bldg.  He was doing business/ insurance in Eastern Washington & Idaho.  Bob was a long time resident and secretary for the Spokane Club.  He was once the receiver for the Spokane Falls, Citizens National Bank, he later resigned due to (bank failure in 1894-1900).  He engaged in various mining endeavors, one of the directors along with J. D. Sherwood and others of the Cork-Province Mines, LTD., located near Kaslo, B. C.  Bob was a director of the Lakeview Mining and Milling Co.  Later he became the secretary and trustee of the (BFC) in 1914 - that same year Mr. Strickland deeded to the Birchwood Farm Co. the fifteen (15) acres, on the southeast side of the highway at the Norman ranch.  R. E. M. Strickland was a member of Regents (1894-1897) duties included - an issuance of a charter, to petition the Board of Regents for museums or historical societies, intent on organizing nonprofit education. [44]

*James Breen portrayed in editorial cartoon/caricature Spokesman Review 1912*

James Breen a well-known smelting, mining engineer and owner of mines, together with the Norman "bros" via hotel chains, and part owner of the BFC, his former residence was the McCornick Building in Utah. [45]

President Ben Norman
Courtesy of Kathleen Beard Birchwood Farm Company

Ben entertains his friends and enjoys a cup of tea in the shade of the old apple tree that he had planted at "Birchwood". His Irish friend Adams (1848-1927) was born in Boston and later graduated from Harvard in 1870. John Adams and John Quincy Adams (penmen) are descendants on the maternal side from the Mayflower crewman John Alden. Adams is best known as a pioneer lawyer, historian and a grandson & great grandson of two U.S. presidents. Adams, A. M. Winston and other high profile Spokane Attorneys counseled before the Interstate Commerce Commission: the City of Spokane (Chamber of Commerce) v. Northern Pacific railway (J. Hill). Senator Miles Poindexter served on the Interstate Commerce. [46]

John Dickinson Sherwood aka "Dicky;" the Spokane Harvard Club president, in 1908 entertained from his Spokane residence, well-known society pioneers, including T. B. Higgins, Charles Frances Adams Jr., and Henry Adams among other club members. J. D. Sherwood was a member of the Hasty Pudding club, the Family Club (Hearst) and (the Bohemian Club & Grove) of Spokane and San Francisco. Mr. Sherwood once served as the pres., of the WWP CO. - SPOKANE STREET RAILWAY, ETC., - and a director of the Spokane and Eastern Trust Co.

In addition; Sherwood was instrumental in helping Kirtland Cutter and Ben Norman purchase a portion of said land at the mouth of Deep Creek (the Inland Railway and Street Co.) for the purpose of the State Park. Agents, W. S. Norman and J. D. Sherwood were heavy partners in the real-estate part of the Spokane Washington Improvement Company allotting the moneys for park purposes. [47]

The Washington Water Power controlled the following companies, which, while separate corporations, are treated as one property: Spokane Street Railway, chartered Dec. 13, 1886. Officers President H. Bolster, Sec., general manager and purchasing agent W. S. Norman, and Treasurer, J. D. Sherwood. Through private stock holders who controlled the (WWP) are the very same - controllers of the (BFC) and the Hotel Spokane Syndicate, and so on. [48]

Mr. Sherwood was the owner of the Los Molinos Land Co. in San Francisco. He was a member of the Zeta Psi Fraternity founded in 1846. Enoik- eteria; Filiki Eteria or *Society of Friends* (Greek: Φιλική Εταιρεία or Εταιρεία των Φιλικών) a secret 19th-century organization. The direct translation of the word 'Filiki' is 'Friendly' and the direct translation of the word 'Eteria' is 'Society' (also *'Company'* or *'Association'*). [49]

Note worthy: 'John Dickinson Sherwood' may likely be related to the 'Founding Father John Dickinson'.

Tragically two Bonesmen; John Dickinson Sherwood, '83, and Charles Mortimer Belshaw, '83, and their wives were killed by accident, in a car crash on November 23rd 1919. The tour car they were driving fell 400 feet down Devil's Slide in San Francisco at Half Moon Bay Rd. From the Grizzly Bear California magazine, a briefing of the article quoted; "At the same time, the lives of his wife Maude (nee Spencer) Belshaw and their guests, Mr. & Mrs. J. D. Sherwood of Spokane were snuffed out. Senator Belshaw was a former past Grand Master of the Native Sons of the Golden West. A relative of the Senator was Richard Rains Veale (Sheriff of Contra Costa), a charter member of the N.S.G.W.

Both, C. M. Belshaw and J. D. Sherwood's wives of noble lineage descend from the Spencer (De Spencer) bloodline. Josephine Belle

Sherwood's father Joseph Spencer Cone descends back to the Norman Conquest, and the British-American Colonies. He is the son of Timothy Cone-one of four brothers East Haddam Massachusetts, who is the son of Joseph Cone. Cone Grove Park (named for Joe Spencer Cone) is located in Red Bluff, California. "At the time of this writing," high radiation levels have been confirmed at Half Moon Bay, California, due to the Fukushima nuclear disaster. [50]

**Note:** Prescott Bush, George Bush H. W. and George W. Bush have all been members who have celebrated the annual bacchanal at Bohemian Grove. See: San Francisco Roster 1892.

## Chapter 12
## Cuprum – Idaho

In 1901 Pete Kramer, ran the horse drawn stage coach line between Council Idaho - Cuprum, and the Seven Devils/Weiser, Salubria and Indian valley stage line-seven to the devils mine-1891. [51]

As outside writers' looking within the official stories written by insiders, from time to time, we came across other parallels between stage coaches. Did earlier historian/historians confuse the Kramer stage line/Seven Devils with that of a parallel story of the Spokane House? In particular, one such parallel between Pete Kramer and "Pea vine Jimmy" Walton's Hotel? Dating from the 1900's the so called stories emerged. Incidentally mixing and merging them, in effect creating the official story known today as the "Pea vine Jimmy," stagecoach line, merchant stores, hotels, taverns, feed stores? The Kramer story coincidentally runs parallel with Walton's story? Both stage lines not only ran through Chattaroy and Cuprum Idaho but along the cottonwood Rd. Additionally stories are interwoven; as such James Walton and Pete Kramer, hotel keepers, stagecoach drivers and mail carriers. [52]

The Black Hills Stage Coach Robberies - Nevada Outback's gold. Pioneer Station Masters – the likes of, Ide, Goodman, and James Walton, or better known as "Pea vine Jimmy." The character known as "Pea vine Jimmy," a "liveryman" had charge of the station in partnership with

Frank Goodman and other English Merchants who came from different directions to meet; set the stage where they meet at the marketplace - a pioneer Dry goods and general merchandise store. [53]

The incorporator's in 1892 of the Spokane and Coeur d'Alene Railway and Navigation are A. A. Newberry, W. S. Norman, James Monaghan, L. C. Dillman, D. M. Drumheller and *C. B. King*, having been formed for the construction of an electric R. R. between the two cities. The Co's HDQRS is located in Spokane. The latter, Mr. King was the owner of the stage line that ran from Colfax to Spokane Falls. [54]

Mining Kings & their Silent Partners; The Walton's had arrived early on in Pennsylvania, aka "the Keystone State". A keystone is a central wedge in an arch that locks all other pieces of an arch in place. It is the part of an arch that all other parts depend upon. We looked in vain for some reference to answer the question of James Walton's origin. To help unlock the secret we used the origin key.

The Byberry Waltons proved to be an interesting read; they first dwelled in caves upon their arrival to Pennsylvania - not unlike the Swedes, and or the Essenes.

Another key to Unlocking the Secret Origin of James' was through his closest relatives with Huguenot/Quaker families via ties with religious affiliation. He was allied by marriage via his younger sister Dorothy Walton Monnett. The Walton's ancestry connects with the Chastain/Chasten, and Ludwigs, just to name a few more prominent families herein - starting a chain reaction which later proved helpful in finding "the others?" Within James' life story there are family connections indicating Masonic origin. In spite of this the answers are still out there in stories like the "Muncy Masons" who settled early on in Pennsylvania. Pieced together and encoded in fragmented clues left behind are scattered sources amply supplied by (Edwards 1900, p. 529), historian Edward Becher, and other historians. However, they reveal only a glimpse into the inscrutable James "Pea vine Jimmy" Walton. For that reason it took some fathoming out and methodical research in an attempt to solve the age-old riddle of Pea vine Jimmy. He was someone who was not well-known, obscure and mysterious, of unimportant standing, an ordinary pioneer mountain man. Edwards described Mr. Walton's character as, "a very pretentious man, not ambitious for leadership, but he was well liked by his neighbors in Chattaroy."

In response to Mr. Edwards's opinion, the author's herein add; unpretentious characteristics do remain of him, a humble log building, known as the "Pea vine Jimmy" monument he allegedly left behind at the Spokane House, presently on the site of a museum. In reality, the mere fact is simply out of character for our mystery man "Pea vine Jimmy." He was not a simple countryman at all, living a common life.

As *a matter of fact; interestingly enough, h*is astrological sign suggests that he was a natural born leader with management skills, and accumulating wealth was within his grasp. Yet, James Walton was no ordinary man. He is an exact opposite of the unpretentious character Jonathan Edwards so described. Such as; James Walton patented the town of Cuprum, Idaho, and was the superintendant of the United Copper mine, see Augustus Heinze.

Even though we think highly of the respected Jonathan Edwards narrative sources and literary words as well as other well-known official historians prior text - in relation to James "Pea vine Jimmy" Walton. With all due respect - those accounts simply do not fit the facts. They were simply unaware of these new found facts that revealed his characteristics and his background. In which case, we have taken the liberty "left open to our own devises" in an attempt to answer these age old questions, we have left no stone unturned in our search for James Walton's mother and father, new clues that ultimately reveal his true-identity. [55]

The two of us worked hard to track down James Walton's actual life story. With limited funds and research access - perception can often be contradictory. We make up for it by having the freedom to express negative and or positive judgments about our subjects. Independently we are counterintuitive and free to self-edit, thereby creating a more objective and realistic approach without bias. Intuition has told us something was amiss, not quite right with the stories up to date. Our personal objective as author's has been to point the way to future researchers and student's alike, who may be able to fill in more blanks for the interest of history.

How come the Benjamin Norman (BFC) is not publicly familiar? Not to mention James Walton, whose background origin seems to have been overlooked? Could the real James Walton have been deliberately obfuscated, and if so why? Who was he really? What identifying qualities and beliefs distinguish him? For one, he was a man with religious convictions. His Quaker roots reveal, a God-fearing man. He was intimately connected with the Moravian missionaries / United Brethren. The settlement was supported by the funds of the society of the U. B. in London. The London association in aid of the missions of the U.B. called Moravians. [56]

After further research, a 'question arose' as to whether on not the Rev. Jonathan Edward's (book History of Spokane County 1900) herein is descended from the theologian and minister Jonathan Edwards (1703-1758), a 1720 graduate of Yale College, whose namesake is the Jonathan Edwards College a residential college at Yale University in New Haven, Connecticut, Skull & Bones Society).

Pea vine Jimmy-The Quaker; - as early as 1853, a mission agency was organized as the "Home, Frontier, and Foreign Missionary Society." Wagon trains of UB pioneers took months of travel from Iowa to Oregon. The purpose of which was to establish United Brethren churches.

Written many years after the events in this; in which case earlier pioneers try to remember and describe details in their personal accounts, relevant to the building/buildings. Curiously, they did not have the foggiest idea who James "Pea vine Jimmy" Walton was? Neither of them was able to recount to Lewis in their memoirs that knew of him. By all accounts, allegedly when James Walton arrived to the Washington Territory – he chose not disclose his true identity. Did his closest friends help to conceal his identity from the public – all the whiles a building receives public attention – manifesting myths to mask his true identity and bloodline?

Only until recently have the author's in this been able to find his death after an exhaustive search as of 2010 up to date. His true identity has been kept concealed before and after death - *hiding him* from the public eye, begging the question, WHY?

One can't help but wonder, if the first name of James Walton is a "Dit" name – in relation to Abel James? Henry Drinker and Abel James, were both members of the Society of Friends/ Quakers, and prominent among the merchants of the town, large importers of dry goods and general merchandise, and owners of vessels used in the ocean carrying trade. Their warehouse was on the river front near Race Street. Henry Drinker was the Clerk of the Monthly Meeting - *Friends* of Philadelphia, a highly esteemed member of the Society, he died in 1809. [57]

Pennsdale, a village in Muncy Township was founded by a group of Quakers in 1799 who built meetinghouses. One of the first meetings was held in Samuel Wallis's home in 1791. "The Plantation Muncy Farms aka Hall's Farms". The nearest Masonic Lodge was in Williamsport, Lycoming, Pennsylvania early on. James Walton is related to Esq. Henry Lenhart (1816-1894) once the Chaplain of Williamsport.

The first Masonic funeral ever witnessed and recorded in Muncy was in 1812. On the open bible lay the emblematic square and compass. Both the square and compasses are architect's tools, a symbol of Freemasonry, used in Masonic ritual as emblems to teach symbolic lessons. [58]
-It's worth a read History of Lycoming County Pennsylvania John F. Meginness-1892.

United Theological Seminary is a United Methodist seminary in Trotwood, Ohio, just outside Dayton in the Dayton metropolitan area. Founded in 1871 by Milton Wright (the father of Orville and Wilbur *Wright*) originally sponsored by the U. B. in Christ Church. In 1946, members of the Church of the U. B. merged with the Evangelical Church to form the Evangelical U. B. Church. When that denomination merged with The Methodist Church in 1968, United Theological Seminary became one of the thirteen seminaries affiliated with the new United Methodist Church. Their agenda was to convert the heathens (the

Natives) from their own religion, into the religion of the missionaries at the time. The Moravian Church of the Unity of the Brethren adopted a church emblem having an open Bible, with a cross behind in the center, and a chalice in front to the left. The Muncy Mason open bible (Freemasonry) is a direct contradiction and a violation, to the U.B., deeply opposed to freemasonry.

The Muncy Masons; Previous heirs of the Holland Land Company sold their land to Samuel Wallis and Henry Drinker, who in turn gave the land to his daughter and son-in-law, Elizabeth and Charles Hall. It is worth a read Abel James and Henry Drinker in relation to the Philadelphia tea-party. They were subservient to the East India Company, at the same time John Dickinson was a Quaker and a penman. "It is most probable that J. D. Sherwood is related to John Dickinson". [59]

## Chapter 13
**Intriguingly striking similarities between Two Walton's...**
**James Walton's** Mtn. ID / **Earl Hamner Jr.,** Walton's Mtn. VA

~ In 1882 James Walton was Kidd/ Chattaroy Washington's first post master.
~ In 1882 Mr. Hamner lived in a community, originally called "Walker's Mill", named for Schuyler George Walker a local mill operator, and first postmaster.

Earl Henry Hamner, Jr. (7-10-1923) was a writer, and is best known for the CBS television series "The Walton's." Earl Jr. passed on March 24th, 2016 marking a turning point in this. Many of the episodes were based on true-stories.

Mr. Hamner was reared on the family homestead in Schuyler Nelson County Virginia by his natural parents Earl Henry Hamner Sr. and Doris Marion (nee Giannini) - notice the maiden name? Is she related to Amadeo Pietro Giannini (1870–1949) founder of the Bank of America – a business partner to Orra E. Monnett?

On a side note; Jean Monnet, aka godfather of the European Union, the Bank of *England* - and Montagu Collet Norman, 1st Baron Norman (1871 – 1950) was an English banker, aka the Governor of the Bank of England from 1920 to 1944. He became a director of the Bank of England in 1907.

In the Walton television series; the character (ma Walton) Olivia welcomes "Friends" and or strangers into her home. She later develops tuberculosis, and enters a sanitarium in Arizona. The Walton-Johnson-Monnett familial ties of Old Virginia suffered from consumption/ tuberculosis in real-life. It has been noted that a familial/ hereditary disease, such as; consumption can appear in individuals by heredity. [60]

The *First* Families of Virginia (FFV) originated with colonists from England, mainly settling at Jamestown and along the James River and other passable waters in the Colony of Virginia during the 17th century. A descendent of any of the men on either list can rightly claim to belong to one of the first families of Decatur County, and so forth, with the same pride as the First Families of Virginia. [61]

Interestingly the surnames, Hamner, Goodman, Kidd and Walton are listed in the: Heads of Families at the First Census of the U.S. taken in the Year 1790. [62]

Might Thomas Walker of the Royal Land Company of Virginia be related to Mary Walker's husband, an early Post Master in Chattaroy, Washington?

See family connections; Kinnear, Monnett, Walker, White, Semmes, *Simpson*.

## Chapter 14
## Walton's Mountain in Idaho

How did the Seven Devils Mountains get its name? Several different versions of the story give credit to the Hudson Bay Co., trappers, Native Americans, old timers, and or early miners. *For what it's worth*, we have varying thesis of our own;

Relative to; Pennsylvania Ohio, Devil's half acre, and devil's cave, the Freemasons put up a lot of monuments, and narratives often run parallel with the biblical stories of Babylonian and Jerusalem.

Such as; Mary Magdalene, Seven devils/ demons, *Cuprum cop*per (Mary Magdalene) lived in *Caupernaum which means Cuprum in Latin*, St. Cyr was a partner of James Walton in the Seven Devils Mountain range. In 1899 James Walton patented and owned the town of *Cuprum*, as placer ground located in the Seven Devils Mining District of Idaho, south of the Buffalo Hump area. The seven Devils are remarkable peaks located within the Idaho district of the Hells Canyon Wilderness with numerous evil peak names. In the region beginning with the two tallest: He Devil, She Devil, Devils Throne, Mt. Belial, The Ogre, Twin Imps and the Goblin, and so on.

When the weather permitted Mr. Walton would send in a six horse team load of mining equipment and supplies, bringing out ore when he left, to take to the nearby smelter. The Kramer Stage Station ran thru the *Council/Cuprum area.* [63]

In addition to the Seven Devils Smelter, James Walton was the superintendant of the United Copper Mines Company. He owned extensive interests in the camp and arrived in Cuprum Saturday last from Weiser with a load of provisions. H. M. St. Cyr associated with Mr. Walton and conferred in New York with members of the United Copper mines company. [64]

Anaconda Copper Mining Company aka the Amalgamated Copper Mining Company was one of the largest trusts of the early 20th century founded in 1881 in connection with Marcus Daly and the trio of Copper Kings. He quickly expanded the company due to the discovery of huge copper deposits. At the beginning of the 1900s, due to electrification (and Amalgamated maintenance of an artificially high copper price), copper was very profitable, and copper mining expanded rapidly. Spanning the years, 1899-1915, Anaconda was controlled by Standard

Oil Trust insiders, namingly of Amalgamated Copper Company. Frank Monnett was the Attorney general for Ohio in 1898, when he took Standard Oil Corp., of Ohio to Supreme Court. See Sherman-Anti Trust - Apex-law 1872; (Wikipedia Commons).

After Marcus Daly died in 1900 his widow partnered with John D. Ryan who became the president of Daly's bank. Ryan took control over Henize's properties, and the properties of William A. Clark. The Rockefellers gained control of Butte's copper when they merged these companies with Amalgamated. In 1909 there was agitation among the shareholders of Heinze's control of the Ohio Copper Company through the company's only lifeline, the Mascotte tunnel.

Senator William Andrews Clark (1839 – 1925), was a Huguenot and the owner of the United Verde Copper Company, w/ traces of some Huguenots late seventeenth-Century Europe, Monet b. Pennsylvania 1839. His daughter Huguette Clark had a large doll collection from France. Was his daughter, Huguette named for Agnes and Huguette for the Waldensians? Huguette dela Cote Jean of Vienne 1321 burned - Joan of Arc.

The Amalgamated Copper Co, (Augustuz Fritz Heinze), a securities-holding corp. for "The American" Copper mine of (James Walton's) interest in the mine. [65]

James Breen was a well-known smelting operator "that is to say" he was widely known for his expertise in smelting ore. With all due respect; James Breen was a "Copper King" of the Pacific Northwest, and with almost certainty he would have known in person James "Pea vine Jimmy" Walton within the mining circles, and other closely identified interests, like freemasonry. James Breen was a friend, close confidante, and a partner of the Norman brothers within the BFC, mining, and a chain of Hotels. Without a doubt James Breen and James Walton stayed at the Numerous Norman hotels during the 1890's. James Breen, James Walton and the Norman brothers intimately connected with the Copper King trio, (William Andrews Clark, Marcus Daly and Augustus Fritz Heinze) of Butte, Montana. In 1890 Elizabeth O'GRADY married Marcus

O'FARRELL the nephew of a 'Copper King' Marcus Daly who was once the president of the Anaconda Copper mine in Montana.

Following the death of Mr. Daly, Elizabeth later married James Breen. United Copper was incorporated in 1902 by F. Augustus Heinze, a *copper magnate* who competed with Amalgamated Copper for lucrative copper mines in Butte, Montana. In 1902 he merged these as the United Copper Company, a short-lived United States copper mining business in the early 20th century that played a pivotal role in the Panic of 1907 - also known as the 1907 Bankers Panic aka Knickerbocker Crisis. Daly developed the Anaconda Mine and smelter operation in partnership with George Hearst, along with other big investors at that time. [66]

A significant economic depression which resulted to widespread bank suspensions was the panics of 1873, 1893, 1907 and a suspension in 1914. *The chaos theory*, in view from another perspective of interconnectedness dates the first worldwide financial crisis in the 1907 bank panic of the falling stock market, which resulted in "the butterfly effect," a great shock to investors worldwide.

James Breen, the owner of the Porphyry Dyke Gold Mining Co., mine in the Rimini country, is also the General Manager in connection with the Anaconda Co. in Helena Montana with Augustus Heinze. [67]

**The Death of James" is new information, and as such; "if a historical text;** discusses old newspaper articles to derive a new historical conclusion, it is then considered to be a **primary source** for the new conclusion, but a **secondary source** of information found in the old documents". [68]

## Chapter 15
## "The Angel of Death Claims James Walton"

The angel of death claimed James Walton, who passed away at the ripe old age of 78. He had initially intended to return to Spokane, Washington in 1908. He arrived at his brother's Martin Van Buren near Kirkpatrick, Ohio in the best of health. However, he failed to recover after being stricken with paralysis. Incidentally he passed away on

December 5th. 1907. He had been under the care of his closest relatives and the family Doctor. James Walton was known as *"Pea vine Jimmy"* to many of the first settlers of the Spokane Territory, he died at his brother's home in Kirkpatrick on a Thursday. He is buried in a cemetery nearby Martin's home in Kirkpatrick.

**The Marion Daily Mirror 1908 James Walton obituary / eulogy describes;**
James Walton died of what the physicians noted as a stroke of paralysis within months following the peak of the worldwide 1907 depression. Due to the Panic of 1907, allegedly that is why President Woodrow Wilson signed into law the Federal Reserve Act. Might the financial crisis within months before James Walton's stroke of paralysis/ panic attack, been a shock, a "trigger," for the stroke? Attributing to the fact that James was heavily invested in *stocks* and mining beforehand? When James arrived at his brother Martins home in Kirkpatrick he was in good health. Shortly thereafter, while still at his brother's, he became incapacitated. Might this have been a nervous breakdown brought on by extreme stress?
**The passing of James Walton from yet another headline article in 1908;** "Mr. James Walton of Spokane may not recover from the shock". "If *words* have *two meanings*, the word 'shock may have meant 'shock of paralysis' in one sense, and 'shock of the stock market' in another". [69]

James Walton was known by the Historical Pioneer Societies who knew him personally as *"Peavine Jimmy."* These are newspaper families privy to records. The Norman, Burnett, Durham, Lewis and Cowles, families descend from Newspaper media publishing families? The extent to which these newspaper families, and early historians are influenced within their own group, a devotion such as; their close connection with the Pioneer Societies, whose agenda, remains the same then and now- which is to write down and record history - often a consideration for debate. For instance; the Norman brothers "Billy and Ben" descend from newspaper families, and were connected in the newspaper / publishing business early on in the Washington Territory, as well as in England, hence; George Norman of the Cheltenham Examiner.

Herein a Historical Society had recognized the appellation, "Jew's Jack Harp," a similar scenario plays out to that of the Steven's County Pioneer Society (*Society of Friends*, Jesuits), easily recognized James Walton as "*Pea vine Jimmy*." As initiates of freemasonry they may well have understood the meaning behind his nickname.

The General Mining Act of 1872 is a United States federal law that authorized and governs prospecting and mining for economic minerals, such as gold, platinum, and silver, on federal public lands. Frank Goodman's claim in the 1873 Old Dominion Mine follows a year after the 1872 - Apex, Law. [70]

Some of the data listed here is a work in progress, and as such: The Marriage Date on April 14, 1899 in the County Courthouse of Record Weiser; Records Idaho for James Walton's marriage to Martha Buffington - she later married Pete Kramer?

**"Bloodlines" link Fuller-White-Monet-Mayflower Pact Connection**; An exodus story revolved around the Monnett family, allied through the marriage of Dorothy and Abraham. They were a devoutly religious family, so it makes sense to include some biblical names; such as, James' name Hebrew or Egyptian origin; James "Pea *Vine* Jimmy" Walton has connections to powerful men, some within his family unit. The Monnet and the White family Vine connect by means of the union of Dorothy and Augustus "Eddy" Monett. Mr. Monnett traces his family lineage back to that of Samuel Fuller," a Mayflower pact signer 11-11-1620. Fuller was involved in the church's decision to move to Northern Virginia per agreement with the Virginia Company. Later on "the Company" Dr. Samuel Fuller became a deacon of the Plymouth church. The "Father of Spokane Parks" Aubrey Lee White is also a "blood relation", of Samuel Fuller, the same kinship as William White. Aubrey White via consanguinity is a distant cousin to "Eddy" Monnett. The Monnett/Money genealogy ancestry traces back to the Kings of the (Magna Carta) to the 12th century. Moneta, Plantagenet, French line dynasties. According to David Icke, a British Author, - many of the celebrities including most of the President's walk the red carpet in much the same way the Royal family does. [71]

"Imagine for the moment" the historical "Pea vine Jimmy" building may have been built by a Frenchman with Noble blood running through his veins?  How much "Sangreal" courses through the Walton-Monnett "bloodline?"  Families of noble French Huguenot descent closely connected to James "Pea vine Jimmy" Walton via his little sister, Anna Dorothy Walton-Monnett family, and the marriage of Thomas F. Johnston and Martha L. (Walton).  Like the Natives, most of the Huguenots in the 21st C. were assimilated into various societies and cultures in America.

**Huguenot Exodus:** The Bible teaches that salvation comes only through faith in Jesus Christ, and that Christians are neither to participate in things done in secret (Eph. 5:10-15) nor to show favoritism (James 2:1). Therefore, United Brethren members must not be members of any other church, group, or organization which teaches a way of salvation incompatible with the United Brethren Confession of Faith, such as a Masonic lodge or the Order of Odd Fellows. Members who do, and who refuse to sever the relationship after having been confronted by the pastor and at least one other board member shall be regarded as having withdrawn their membership from the church. (John 14:6, 2 Corinthians 6:14-15). [72]

Interestingly; William C. Walton follows along a similar story as James "Pea vine Jimmy" Walton, in that he was a post master, merchant, etc, in Virginia.

The Huguenots continued migrating to America throughout the mid-18th Century most of their congregations gradually absorbed into the Episcopal Church.

The burning bush has been a popular symbol among Reformed churches since it was first adopted by the Huguenots (French Calvinists. The motto; I am burned but not consumed.  However, given the fire is a sign of God's presence, he who is a consuming fire (Hebrews 12:29) the miracle appears to point to a greater miracle: God in grace is with his covenant people and so they are not consumed. Symbol a burning bush *Jacques Le Moyne* de Morgues, A *Huguenot* Artist, went to Roanoke Colony, where he was a friend of Sir Walter Raleigh. How many Huguenot's may have fled to Roanoke Colony to escape the edict? When the White finally arrived on the mysterious lost Colony of Roanoke Island, Virginia on August 18, 1590, he found the colony abandoned and looted, with no trace of the settlers. It is interesting to note; the Huguenot cross; Maltese cross and the Knights templar cross are similar in design.

On Wednesday the 31st of December in the year 1687, the first French Huguenots left the Netherlands for the Cape, with *Vine* shoots from France with them on the ship. The Jewish nation is represented under the symbol of a vine.

Orra Eugene Monnett was a member of numerous Masonic Fraternities. If one is interested in his Family Genealogy: See; an emphasis of a noble Huguenot heritage somewhat of the first immigrants "Issac and Pierre Monnet." You will learn about the Persecution of Hugeunots/ the Waldensians in the Massacre of Merindol in 1545. The Heresy of the the Waldensian Movement Witches. [73]

How James Walton acquired his nickname "Pea vine Jimmy" is fuzzy; the reason behind A. J. Wyatt's fraternity name "Jews Jack Harp" is more obvious? A livery stable sign hung in the early mining days of Idaho, pioneer stables kept by "Jews Harp Jack" and "Web-Foot Haley". One corner of the sign painted a Jews Jack Harp; opposite corner a massive foot with webs between the toes. Haley came from Willamette Valley Oregon. [74]

The Latin name of James is Jacobus – from the time of the Stuart Exile – Jacobites – Royal Society – Jacobites French Freemasonry. The name origin for (James is a Supplanter) seizing by the heel; -- one who illegally seizes and holds the place of another; -- a Squatter someone who settles on land without right or title.

Theirs Power in a Name; the way in which James Walton took his initiate/adept nickname "Pea vine Jimmy" hints; of freemasonry and religious connotations. Mr. Walton is a generational Quaker, and as such the name "James" comes after a very curious evolution, from the Hebrew name Jacob. When in Greek times people were named after Jacob — the arch-father of Israel — they were given the Hellenized version Jacobos (Iakobos). Hence there are four men in the Bible called Jacobos (James): Was Jacobean - Jacobin – Jacobite. These three words all start the same, because they all derive from the Latin form (Jacobus) of the name James. Another example is that God, and Jesus did rename some of the disciples such as; Simon, (whom he also named Peter), and Andrew his brother, James and John, Philip and Bartholomew. Luke 6:14

**As far as nicknames are concerned, the act of renaming is not new;** according to Brian Heatley (born 1968), aka Michael Tsarion, (Genesis 35:9) reveals a clever ploy by bible mythographers to distort history & obscure the identity & existence of the Cult of Aton.

On another note; a sobriquet, and or myth might be fabricated to minimize the significance of something by explanation: The Hudson Bay Company is better known, without revealing to much about James "Pea vine Jimmy" Walton, who thus far been obfuscated, and overshadowed by the better known HBC. To date, the public/reader knows very little about James Walton, because the historians know little about him. For clues we looked behind the pseudonym, within mythology, religion, and of course the philosophy, of language of freemasonry. After all, his entire life story is shrouded in mystery. The meaning behind his uncommon nickname "Pea vine Jimmy" is left open to interpretation. A few historians have speculated on how he acquired an alias, but we don't agree with any them, they don't seem to fit his character.

**Just for fun, we have listed a few of our hypothesis to his nickname;**
A. J. Wyatt arrived in Weiser Idaho with the first wagon load of ore ever hauled from the Seven Devils District, and wagons of ore from the "Blue Jacket" copper mine, Cuprum Idaho. The Black Hills fever broke out. Many miners made preparations to start new diggings. A. J. Wyatt "Jews Harp Jack" rented a farm on Dry Creek, Eldorado. Most likely Frank Goodman & James Walton stayed at his ranch? [75]

Another clue "saving the best for last," is how James Walton received his nickname "Pea vine Jimmy," in the first place. It may have had something to do with; Anneas Wyatt and his (Will & Testament, dated March 1911). Wyatt bequeaths his placer homestead land to James Walton, (a close friendship between Wyatt and Walton).
"Just maybe, Anneas Wyatt is related to Sir Frances Wyatt (1588-1644) the first English royal governor of the Virginia Colony/the Company"? [76]

U. B. Brethren (decipher Huguenot code); thus far, the up to date narratives; about "Pea vine Jimmy" have been hazy, creating a disillusion making his identity indistinct, by preferring to call him by his alias "Pea vine Jimmy". A key factor is his Quakerism roots; which can tell a lot about his religious convictions. Identification of the most likely origin of the alias closely associated with "Peavine Jimmy," so nicknamed because of the initiation of an adept in California. We searched for an obvious question of how James Walton was initiated into the mysteries and sacred rites, a secret order, from "The Pasteboard Fraternity of California", and dubbed into symbolic Masonic nomenclature, "is (Pea vine Jimmie) named after a wild-flower"? "Not so fast". James may have lived under many aliases in various places while prospecting. In Washington State he is best-known as "Pea vine Jimmy," the obvious reason being the "Pea vine Jimmy" building.
Placer miners of the Idaho mines were initiated/ initium into the "Pasteboard fraternity in California". For the most part, the old timers of California were re-christened by their constituents or patrons. Among them was Anneas Wyatt, who was re-christened as "Jew's Jack Harp," amongst his initiate friend "Pea vine Jimmy." However, a true tale remains untold, as is often the case among the mysteries of freemasonry. The reason being that John W. Wells an Indian Agent of Jocko Agency, who once lived in the Montana Terr., passed away in Washington County Idaho. He took his own life, before he could complete, and later reveal the rest of an unidentified initiation list he'd compiled. The list is too long to insert here, and contains about 63 initiate names more or less, probably shy about 40 names that remain nameless because of the sad incident that Mr. Wells inflicted upon himself. [77]

Daniel Galeucia, a roommate to James Walton in their later years, the two lived in Chattaroy, where sadly Mr. Galeucia would take his own life. [78]

It is worth noting here; a letter was sent to the Hon. N. J. Taylor (Indian Affairs) signed by John Wells (U. S. Indian agent). The "Burline" Grist & Sawmill erected on the Jaco River, two miles east of the Flathead agency runs along a parallel story to the (Yantis & Chief Garry's grist mill). [79]
See; Montana Fish and Wildlife & Parks Jocko River Trout Hatchery

The objectives of the Society of California Pioneers 1850 Articles of Incorporation; was dedicated to the study of California art, history, and culture. The Membership was opened to first family descendants of pioneers (ffv) who arrived in California prior to Jan. 1, 1850.

Perhaps James Walton himself or even his closest friends tried to mask aspects of his background. After all, his identity, and place of origin have been unknown for some time. Did they pull off some kind of ruse, to hide him, obscuring his true identity? Various reasons give way to why James may have had a penchant for secrecy. He may have withheld his identity to unknown individuals, if he had felt threatened in any way. If a person was of Huguenot descent, one might attempt to lessen that risk through anonymity. The Huguenots were persecuted so harshly, that they needed to choose a safe place to live from the outsider's in the world. The fact of the matter remains that the Huguenots ultimately ended up having all their civil liberty rights taken away, one only has to read the Massacre of Merindol in 1545. They retained the religious provisions of the Edict of Nantes until the rule of Louis XIV, who progressively increased persecution of them until he issued the Edict of Fontainebleau (1685), which abolished all legal recognition of Protestantism in France, forcing the Huguenots to convert. [80]

Poeville / Pea vine Peak on Peavine Mountain is located in Washoe County Nevada, where a small mining camp organized in 1863. Early prospectors discovered wild pea *vines* growing in a place named "*Pea* vine Springs," perhaps another clue behind James Walton's nickname "Pea vine Jimmie."

**Still a work in progress in this;** Sir George Simpson, was the Governor-in-Chief of the Hudson's Bay Company. During this period (1820-1860) he practiced law for "Rupert's Land". Geddes Mackenzie Simpson (1775-1848), in connection with his uncle's firm merged with that of Andrew Colvile in 1812. Simpson came into contact with the Hudson's Bay Co. since Colville was a director of the (HBC) and the brother-in-law of Thomas Douglas, 5th Earl of Selkirk. In 1820 Colville appointed him Governor-in-Chief, of Rupert's Land. In which Colville W.T., is named. The Simpsons were farmers and large slave owners. [81]

Isabel G. Simpson was born in the Rocky Mountain region of Colorado. She married Jacob Beard, of Trinidad, Colorado. We wonder if Harold Beard herein may be a descendent of Jabob Beard.

Raphaeletta Semmes Simpson - member of the N.S.D.A.R.; b. March, 1870, in Denver, Colo., m. June 12, 1890, in Trinidad, Colo. Burgess Lee Gordon, b. 1864, in Frankford, Pike County.

Sir Francis Wyatt (1588–1644) was appointed Governor. In 1625 he was appointed Secretary of State for the colony. His great-grandfather Thomas Wyatt allegedly had a relationship with *Anne Boleyn.*

Raphael Semmes was a midshipman's appt. from then Pres. John Quincy Adams in 1826. Semmes married Anne Elizabeth Spencer in 1837, and furthermore was assigned to Pensacola Navy Base, where he invested in land and slaves in Alabama - See; Amistad. [82]

George Semmes Simpson built the old Fort and Trading Post, where the City of Pueblo now stands; in 1866, settling in Trinidad, where he passed away in 1885; his tomb was cut into solid rock positioned atop the mountain north of Trinidad, aka "Simpson's Nest." Harry Simpson Calkins and Dr. Simpson could be related via Son of Burgess Lee and Ralphaleta (Simpson) Gordon. Burgess Lee Gordon/ Monnett's are related to George Semmes Simpson, a descendent of the Kinnears. They are Virginia cousins (ffv). The first families of Virginia may not be first in order of appearance but are first rank (hierarchy/noble birth). Lewises and Meriwethers derive from French Huguenots/Plantaganet and their kin, Semmes, Gordon are related. [83]

For further study, it is worth a read; The Ft. Pueblo Trading Post, first gold discovery Colorado, Simpson's Rest Trinidad, Colorado.

Another question arose; since the Walton family has close familiar ties that bind to the Durham's via Ida Durham Walton. Might "Pea vine Jimmy" be related to Nelson Wayne Durham? After reading the trio of antique leather bound books written by the notable N. W. Durham; Pres. of the Spokane Historical Society in 1916, Headquarters w/ the Old Spokane Public Library. It is curious as to why Durham made no mention of James "Pea vine Jimmy" Walton within his book trio? The Historical Society agenda is today, the same as it was then, which was to collect manuscripts and genealogies. Other officers of the Society in 1916 include none other than vice-pres., W. S. Lewis, corresponding secy., B. L. Gordon, treasurer and trustee and Jonathan Edwards just to name a few. We're begun to wonder if William S. Lewis might be related to Meriwether Lewis. Recommended Reading; "Lewises, Meriwethers and Their Kin" by Sarah Travers Lewis Scott Anderson.

**N. P. R. R. Railroad Land Lots change hands with a pattern that repeats itself;**

Along a similar 'vine' as the reputed first families of Virginia, the (ffv) families in this research project followed the same pattern as well, with the first families property rights in the order of rank of hierarchy or noble 'bloodlines'.

Dr. Burgess Lee Gordon, M. D., was born in Spokane (1892-1984) later a 1912 Gonzaga University graduate. At one time he attended the Jefferson Medical College in 1919. He was a wholesale grocer, a scientific farmer, and an inventor of the Gordon stethoscope and electric thermometer. His mother was related to Dr. Simpson-St. Louis/Simpson's forceps-childbirth, Uncle Dr. Semmes-surgeon confederate army-civil war.

Jules Lyle Prickett, one of the incorporators of the W.W.P., and a Banker married Mary Estelle Sherlock on Sept. 28, 1892. Mary is the sister of Aimee (Sherlock) Norman. The Prickett's residence was located at 825 W. Seventh Avenue close to his brother in law, William Normans home. J. L. Prickett was a prominent representative of mining interests in Spokane early on. Mr. Prickett organized and became the largest stockholder of the Spokane Savings Bank and was one of the original organizers and stockholders of the W.W.P. Co. Mr. Prickett, was a pioneer charter member of the Spokane Club (Pres. 1896-98).

Note; "Martha Washington is related to John Prickett via Patrick Henry m. Sarah Shelton/ Dorothea Dandridge". See; the Virginia landed gentry.

Kathleen, Louise Elizabeth Prickett and Marjorie Norman Hawkins are the great grandchildren of Samuel and Rosetta Sherlock, Portland, Oregon merchant pioneers. Marjorie married Mark D. Hawkins (1884-1969). Louise Elizabeth Pricket, daughter of Jules Lyle and Mary Estelle (Sherlock) Prickett. Kathleen and Marjorie are Aimee Louise (Sherlock) and W. S. Norman's daughters. [84]

Oregon Pioneers; Samuel F. Sherlock was born in Ireland (1820-1876) to the parents of John and Dorothea Sherlock. Samuel married Miss Rosetta D. (Wale) on 1846 in Wales of Irish descent. His young wife left the luxury of her beautiful English home and traveled abroad from England to New York in 1851, residing there for six years. They traveled by way of the Isthmus with their two young children, (one of the two children was Sarah Francis Sherlock) sailing by ocean to Portland, Oregon in 1857. The couple had two sons and four daughters. William Sherlock a native of Ireland arrived in 1850 with his family crossing the plains to Oregon. William together with Chas. P. Bacon established the "Blackhawk" livery stable in Portland. Mr. Sherlock and C. P. Bacon were both early pioneers who purchased property in Portland, Oregon before 1852. The Sherlock's were early Portland pioneers of the city who platted the Sherlock addition owning extensive property and beautiful homes in Oregon. Samuel Sherlock with his brother William founded the first saddlers shop, S. Sherlock & Co. 52 Front Street in Portland, Oregon.

Mr. Sherlock's faith was within the Episcopal Church (M. E.), a leader in the Masonic fraternity. Sadly he passed away in 1876 from injuries resulting from being thrown from a horse. George Lawrence was a Portland pioneer since 1874 and former partner and brother in law of

Samuel Sherlock.  Mr. George Lawrence and Rose D. *Sherlock* Lawrence married on August 13, 1861, and had children of their own.

The Samuel Sherlock Company is now the George Lawrence Wholesale Saddle Co. [85]

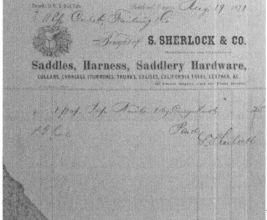

Berg's doc,
Original Primary Source Document:  S.SHERLOCK & CO.
Portland, Oregon, Aug. 19, 1871
Note:  the above left corner, 'Payable in U. S. Gold Coin'

Frances Terbell sold his historical property to J. L. Prickett in 1904, who in turn sold to Ferdinand E. Libenow one year later those same Lots were sold to R. J. Hurd. Ferdinand E. Libenow (1863-1916) was a miner, a Spokane resident and a resident of Canada.  F. E. Libenow was an inventor, and had filed for a Lantern patent and a wash pail patent.  He was appt. an American Consular Agent at Chanaral Chile.  Mr. Libenow was a close *friend* of Spokane Congressman Miles Poindexter (Huguenot), an attorney who served as the assistant prosecuting attorney for Spokane County (1898-1904) as a judge of the superior court from (1904-1908) a Congressman, a Senator and a U. S. Ambassador to Peru, the son of Ferdinand Francis Libenow. [86]

George Poindexter was of (French <u>Huguenot</u> and English ancestry), and the immigrant founder in America settling in the Virginia Colony because of the Revocation of the Edict of Nantes.  The Poindexters descend directly from the Grainville branch of the "old families" in Jersey Island manor house of Grainville for numerous centuries.  Criss Cross a Colonial style brick house built about 1690 by George Poindexter in New Kent County, Virginia, and was listed on the National Register of Historic Places in 1973.

In 1910 Mr. Hurd and his wife Carrie sold Spokane River lots (4 & 5) including a portion of Lot three (3) to H. L. Moody.  In 1911 Mr.

Moody sold some of his little Spokane River Government Lots to Frank M. Hoskins who in turn sold to Henry Horn. One year later Henry Horn sold a portion of his lot/lots on the Spokane River to Dr. Burgess L. Gordon in 1912. Burgess Lee Gordon came to Spokane in 1890. He operated a store once located at the corner of Division and Harrison streets. In 1909 B. L. Gordon purchased a home located at 601 West Seventh Avenue, located within a block of W. S. Norman's manor once located at 644 W. 7th nearby F. Lewis and Winifred Clark's mansion at 601 W. 7th an area known as Marycliff. [87]

Surprising "bloodlines" of the **Rockwood** family records;

David Vaughan Icke was born in 1952, an English writer and public speaker. In all seriousness he has quoted; that if we trace the "bloodline" families back far enough, we get witchcraft. Simply out of curiosity we researched some surnames. From the same book are some notable Foote descendents in our research; We noted *Stillman Foote* who married *Lovica Donaghy* on Feb. 6, 1787, of Sheffield Mass.

One of their daughters Lovica was born on (5-11-1793), she marries Cephas L. Rockwood b. (3-12-1786) on Oct. 20, 1816. Sarah Ellen Rockwood b. (11-15-1825) married on Feb. 7th 1848 Jos. L. Moore. Of their children our main interest herein are two boys who move to the Washington territory early on, Frank R. Moore and Frederick M. Moore are descendents of Nathaniel Foote.
Rebecca was born about 1634, she later married Lieut. Philip. Rev. "Cotton Matther says Philip was murdered with in hideous witchcraft." He died on Jan. 1685. She then married her second husband on Oct. 2, 1688 Major Aaron Cook.

The book contents include wills to descendents; heirs that inherited vast amounts of land, mills, money, and so forth. Many early colonial families had the misfortune of being intertwined in the witchcraft cases. As far as the involvement of Rebecca, "this may have been a case of greed, for land, money and what have you"?

Note; The Rev. D. S. Tuttle is related to numerous noteworthy Americans, and is also a descendent of Nathaniel Foote; and as such; he is related to Frank Rockwood Moore and Frederick M. Moore of Spokane, Washington. Daniel Tuttle married Harriet Francina Foote on Sept. 12th 1865, a daughter Rev. George Foote. She is the only one of six siblings to survive. [88]

In 1878 Frank Rockwood Moore and his wife Sarah Francis "Fanny" (Sherlock) Moore (1853-1941), arrived to Spokane from Portland. Sarah Francis is the 2nd daughter of Samuel and Rosetta Sherlock. She is the sister of Aimee (Sherlock) Norman. Frank Rockwood Moore (1852-1895), was a charter member and a vice-pres. of the Spokane Club early on. At that time the Lamona building adjoined the Spokane Hotel. Frank Rockwood Moore was one of seven "the originals," who chartered/incorporated Spokane Falls in 1881. Mr. & Mrs. Moore purchased Spokane Lots located on the South Hill at 525 W. Seventh in 1884. In 1889, architects Cutter and Malmgren complete the Frank Rockwood Moore dream home. K. K. Cutter also designed a house located at W. 507, 7th Ave. for his ex father in law (D. C. Corbin) and the Austin Corbin house located at W. 815, 7th Ave. These houses still situate at the Corbin & Moore-Turner Heritage Gardens. [89]

Land scrip was a right to purchase federal public domain land in the United States, a common form of investment in the 19th century. As a type of federal aid to local governments or private corporations, Congress would grant land in lieu of cash. Most of the time the grantee did not seek to acquire any actual land but rather would sell the right to claim the land to private investors in the form of scrip. Often the land title was finalized only after the scrip was resold several times. These grants came often came in the form of railroad land grants. The stocks confirm that the holder or bearer is entitled to receive something (such as a fractional share of stock or an allotment of land). [90]

In turn the above property lots two (2) five (5) and six (6) sold in 1936 to the Terminal Storage Company, purchased from Charles G. Gordon son of B. L. Gordon. This property changed hands several times, presently the Boat Launch Area at the little Spokane, is located at Nine Mile, Washington, presently owned by Riverside State Park. This same property passed into succession to W. S. Norman following Ben's death. In 1941 William deeded this portion to his wife Aimee, the same fifteen

(15) acres that R.E.M. Strickland deeded in 1914 to the Birchwood Farm Company.

This property runs along the east side of the road heading north from Spokane House. In 1952 Harold A. Clark and his wife, purchased the Birchwood Farm land from the Grantors, Kathleen N. Calkins, a widow and Mark and Marjorie Hawkins, his wife, excepting 10 acres & Ben Norman's original farm house.

In 1979 the Clark's sold the above property to Maloney and O'Neil, who in turn sold the above property to the Washington State Park. [91]

R. J. Hurd grew world record breaking Burbank potatoes on his farm property on the little Spokane River, Nine Mile, in 1908. R. J. Hurd owned a men's clothing store on the first floor of the Fernwell Building, named for Fernwell Hyde situated Downtown Spokane at 505 W. Riverside Ave - originally known as the Chamber of Commerce. The top two floors were initially used as a hotel. Herman Preusse built the bldg., the same architect who originally designed the Spokane Hotel. [92]

Two pioneer bankers resided on the bank of the Little Spokane River; Benjamin Norman, and John Binkley who sat on the bench for one year. In 1856 John W. Binkley was born in Canada. He later married Josephine Clarkson (1855-1885). John Binkley was admitted to the Tacoma bar in 1883 and afterward joined together with his Canadian cousin Jacob R. The Frank *Bartlett House* built in 1883 a Registered National Historic Place. The two cousins practiced as attorneys in "Proctor in Admiralty" (Maritime Law) in the Bartlett Building in Port Townsend, Washington Territory. The Binkley's in the company of Mr. Taylor removed to Spokane Falls, Washington Territory in 1883. Binkley and Taylor opened a law office together, and organized the Northwestern and Pacific Mortgage Company a year later. Judge Binkley served one year as Spokane County probate in 1885. [93]

J. R. Taylor was a prominent Mason in the Spokane Lodge, No. 34, F. & A.M.; Spokane Chapter No. 2, R.A.M.; Cataract Commandery, No. 3, K.T. He was a thirty-two second degree mason in Oriental

Consistory, No. 2, Scottish rite and belonged to El Katif Temple of the Mystic Shrine. It is note worthy that the Scottish rites of freemasonry members of higher degree are given special knowledge and authority beyond that given to the lower degrees. [94]

In 1883 Herman A. Van Valkenburg a Dutch businessman came to Spokane to appraise railroad investments and form the Northwestern & Pacific Mtg. Co., employed John W. Binkley and Jacob R. Taylor for years as its confidential/secret agents and attorneys. Binkley's business was located at "5-8 Van Valkenburg Bldg., Spokane, Washington. (MAC) Museum

The Northwestern and Pacific Hypotheek Bank, a Holland institution was followed by the North Pacific Loan and Trust Co., in 1889 of which Mr. Binkley was president and occupied his time in farm mortgages. Robert Insinger was the general manager of the NW&PH Bank as of 1908. R. Insinger married Miss Julia Nettleton, the daughter of the Hon. William Nettleton, who owned the Nettleton Addition. [95]

Mr. Binkley was the initial proprietor of the Montvale Hotel in 1899 located at 1001 W. 1st. Avenue downtown Spokane, Washington. The Montvale Hotel was a Single Room Occupancy Hotel. In the early 1900's SRO Hotels were built to sustain the mining and building boom in Spokane. Storefronts were situated on the main floors. The upper floor bedrooms accommodated the smelter men, miners and laborers coming to Spokane for jobs.
Mr. Binkley served as Pres. of the 1st and 2nd fruit fairs of Spokane. John W. Binkley (Montvale farm), Thomas Stuart Griffith a Montana man (Glen Tana farm), W. S. Norman (Birchwood Farm Norman Ranch) and others were organizers of the Spokane Industrial Expositions where livestock and vast mineral exhibits were shown. L. K. Armstrong (Editor, publishing at the Hyde Block) was the superintendent of the mineral Department of the Spokane Industrial Exposition. [96]

In 1914 the Binkley's moved from their Spokane South hill home, to their country home located on the little Spokane River, just upriver from the Norman ranch. John Binkley built a bridge behind his house, to cross the little river.

Montvale Farm, Birchwood Farm, Waikiki Dairy Farm, Flower Field and the Glen Tana Dairy Farm, we're nearby each other along the little Spokane. B. L. Gordon's fish hatchery bordered between Waikiki, Glen Tana and the Flower Field property. Just upriver on the little Spokane from Waikiki and Glen Tana adjoins the Spokane Country Club. In 1928 Mr. Binkley deeded the Montvale property to his daughter Ethylene and her husband Aubrey Lee White. Etheyln and Aubrey lived at Montvale Farm until 1943. Michael Weaver is presently the owner and resident of the Montvale property listed on the Spokane Historical Register. John Binkley was a member of the chamber of commerce. In social circles he belonged to the Spokane Club, the Athletic Club and the Spokane Country Club.

**Indian Painted Rocks;** John Binkley acquired the Indian Painted Rocks property located about two miles upriver from the mouth of the Spokane and the little Spokane River in 1897. J. W. Binkley was known as an ardent hunter and fisherman, "one can only imagine" Theodore (Teddy) Roosevelt, Senator Miles Poindexter and other prominent pioneer European Brother masons in recreation gathering together here at Montvale Ranch in the early years. This area was once heavily populated before the Hudson Bay Company by a band or bands of hunter gatherers, ancestral Native Americans who hiked, hunted and fished here. The above rock art or pictographs depict ancient hunting grounds of the Native American's. They believed the sun, rain, and other forces were controlled by spirits. In religion they worshiped mother earth, animals, plants, the sun, rain, and wind. In ceremonies and prayers they tried to gain the favor of these gods. What tales were told here, what rituals or ceremonies were performed is up to debate, because the Native American's today do not recognize the painted rocks. "Echo"

John Binkley said the painted rocks are a dull red, or terra cotta, color and where not weather-washed are as plain as when put there. "A painter once said to me these people knew how to mix up paint that would stand the test of time." They are on flat granite surface under an overhanging rock and somewhat hard to photograph.
Mr. Binkley stated "he had in his office then and later, a very bright, young clerk of a romantic nature and predilection for Native American's.

When Harry took his holidays, he donned buckskin, and with his pan, bacon and flour, took his camera and sought an Indian camp. He was much interested in the paintings and tried to get information concerning them. His faculty of gaining the confidence of the red men resulted in some very fine Indian photos and the following legend about the painting.

Chief Enoch of the Spokane Indians, residing on the big river just below where the little Spokane unites with it, told him that the paintings were there as far back as the time of his father's great-grandfather, but that they did not know who put them there; that the Indian trail up the little Spokane from the big river ran within twenty feet or so of the paintings; that long ago there stood a large, pine tree close to the painted rocks and when passing if they gave a halloo, it would be answered by an echo, and the Indians believed it to be the abode of the great spirit, and on occasion used to gather there for the purpose of worship. Later this tree was struck by lightning and blown down. After that there was no answering echo and the Indians supposed the Great Spirit had been driven out or destroyed. [97]

Attorney William S. Lewis wrote a monograph "the case of Spokane Chief Garry," coincidentally he also wrote the papers, with a similar dialogue as told by the Burnett brothers, Benjamin Norman amongst others about the Native Americans, the HBC and buildings. Therefore, was Lewis in a situation or a position of power within the official capacity of the "establishment" to derive personal benefit or gain, as a result of Lewis' actions, and decisions as was working at the same time, both an Attorney and Corresponding Secretary of the Spokane Historical Society of Spokane Washington? A possible conflict of interest arises, the agenda of two different parties. One of which may have an influence in keeping with the official history?

A possible scenario; James Walton may have continued to remain in the shadows, as an influence of the edict of Nantes. The Edict of Nantes, signed in April 1598 by King Henry IV of France, granted the Calvinist Protestants of France substantial rights in the nation, which was still considered essentially Catholic at the time. Some of these Missionaries were descendents of the Huguenot survivors.

"We get it, while 'at the same time' fails to understand how some of those same missionaries could have unjustly inflicted upon the Native tribes a double standard. In turn the U. B. was doing the same thing that was unfairly done to them. In attempting to 'undue' a century's old spiritual culture of the Natives they viewed as heathens. The U. B. missionaries supported the Native's conversion to Christianity.

Metaphorically speaking; the Parable of David's son James Walton runs along a similar parable of the "Hidden Seed." Meaning; The Christian David of the Moravian church/ unity of the brethren; Pea vine Jimmy, son of David was born to early German Pennsylvania parents. The identity of "Pea vine Jimmy" is similar to the "Hidden Seed," (a hidden name, a hidden vine.) James Walton attended the United Walton/ M. E. Church. He was characterized by a wealthy family.
"First form" and "original pattern" are *similar* but their usages are drastically different. We observed striking similarities where the land changes hands in a pattern, parallels not unlike the "prototypes" first families of Virginia, (ffv) and so on. Many of these persons derive from religious groups that suffered from religious persecution, leaving their true life stories behind detailed personal accounts. One such example; In 1626, Henri 11, of Bourbon, Prince de Conde laid siege to the Huguenot city of Realmont. The besiegers intercepted a coded letter leaving the city. Rossignol, then a 26-year-old mathematician, had a local reputation for his interest in cryptography. He quickly broke the Huguenot cipher, revealing a plea to their allies for ammunition to replenish the city's almost exhausted supplies. The next day, the besiegers presented the clear text of the message to the commander of Réalmont, along with a demand for surrender: the Huguenots surrendered immediately. {The above code is only one of many used throughout history. Maybe some of the history or rites were encrypted with the pigpen cipher (sometimes referred to as the Masonic/freemason cipher) in keeping their records of history and rites private}. [98]

**Aubrey Lee White a Mayflower Direct Descendant;** The first governing document of Plymouth Colony was the Mayflower Compact, written by the male passengers of the Mayflower. The gentleman consisted mainly of separatist Congregationalists, referring to themselves as "Saints", adventurers and tradesmen, or by the Separatists as

"Strangers", and later referenced as Pilgrims or Pilgrim Fathers. The Separatists fled religious persecution by King James of England. The Pilgrims while on board the ship signed the Mayflower Compact on November 11, 1620 by the Pilgrims. Signing the covenant were 41 of the ship's 101 passengers, while the Mayflower was anchored in what is now Provincetown Harbor within the hook at the northern tip of Cape Code. On August 18, 1587 John White became a grandfather. "Eleanor, daughter to the governor and wife to Ananias Dare, was delivered of a daughter in the Roanoke colony. The child was the first Christian borne in Virginia and as such she was named Virginia. Susannah Fuller, the wife of William White (Mayflower Signer) was the mother of Peregrine White. Aubrey Lee White is a direct descendent of Peregrine White, the first-born English child to the Pilgrims on the Mayflower in America in 1620. [99]

A few interesting perspectives follow; Jacques Le Moyne de Morgues, A Huguenot Artist, went to the Roanoke Colony. He was a friend of Sir Walter Raleigh. How many huguenots fled to Roanoke Colony to escape the edict of nantes? An interesting read is the mysterious Lost Colony of Roanoke.
-Many scholars believe the Merovingian's are the descendants of Jesus and Mary Magdalene, the French noble family in the 13th century. Merovingian Kings started feudalism let their counts/knights Cathars. [100]

The co-authors herein can't help but wonder, could James Walton be connected to the famous "Walton" Gold mine in Virginia in the Louisa County area? The Goodwin tract was taken over by The Old Dominion Chemical Company, of Yorktown, Va., has been chartered, with $275,000 capital. N. Y. The fact is that, James Walton's mother's first name is Louisa. (A descendent of any of the men on either list can rightly claim to belong to one of the first families of Decatur County with the same pride as (FFV) First Families of Virginia).

Another interesting side note: the Tau cross, the Huguenot Society of the Virginia cross, Cross of Languedoc, Virginia Cross, Huguenot cross, Maltese cross, and Knights Templar Cross share a similar design on their flags.

K. K. Cutter designed a beautiful English Estate where J. P. Graves (Waikiki Dairy) and Thomas Stuart/Stewart Griffith of (Glen Tana Dairy) were breeding registered Jersey cattle.  Mr. Griffith was well-known for his registered collies at the famous Glen Tana kennels, and for his store "Benham & Griffith Company".

One of the Native's most prized possessions was their horses, but they'd never seen the likes of the horses of the British settlers who brought horses and horse racing to America.  Every Saturday, Thomas Griffith held private horse racing at the Glen Tana farm was strictly by initiation only into the obscure group.  The neighboring "Birchwood" farm was a retreat for high level freemasons & initiates placed in positions of power, well protected from exposure by the brotherhood.  The Club was privy to lavish hunting parties and sport fishing.  The 'old timers' who visited "Birchwood" were ardent sportsmen and experts in hunting dogs.

Thomas Stuart Griffith was once Director of the Chamber of Commerce, they organized behind the scenes - in a little backroom within the Spokane Hotel after the big 1889 fire.  In the early years (1892) the Spokane Mining exchange and the Chamber of Commerce occupied rooms adjoining offices in the hotel.  The Chamber of Commerce was once known as a Board of Trade before the great fire.  W. H. Taylor was the president of the Board of Trade and W. S. Norman served three years as secretary.   In the early days Mr. Griffith was Vice-President.  A. A. Newberry was the president and Mr. Reeves was secretary. Griffith reserved a room & office in the Spokane Hotel and the Northern Pacific Station situated near-by.  Newberry was one of the heavy stock holders early on in the Hotel Spokane.  In 1890 A. A. Newberry was a charter member and the first president of the Spokane Club in the 621 Columbia Bldg.,Lamona Block adjoining the Spokane Hotel, Spokane, Wash. [101]

Binkley & cousin Jacob, the partners founded Northwestern and Pacific Mortgage Co. in 1886, which merged with Hypotheekbank of Holland in 1896, with Binkley overseeing legal matters. At the turn of the century the two partners founded North Pacific Loan and Trust Co. and loaned a great deal of money for development of commercial and farming interests throughout the region.  Hypotheekbank along with Binkley and

Taylor are recognized in several historic accounts as having had a major role in fueling the city's most prolific building boom from 1900 to 1910.

Binkley and Taylor were significant in helping establish Fort George Wright military post by personally donating $8,000 worth of land in 1896 toward the eventual construction of the post along the Spokane River the next year.

Mr. and Mrs. Calkins and their daughters Miss Kathleen, Miss Mary Louise, and Miss Harriet, and son, John Bartlett Calkins resided at W. 919 12th. In earlier times during the summer months Spokane's socialites, Kathleen (Norman) Calkins and her husband Harry Simpson Calkins amongst their children lived in Ben's bungalow at Birchwood. Kathleen (Norman) Calkins was the daughter of well-known Spokane pioneers W. S. Norman and Aimee L. (Sherlock) Norman.

Miss Kathleen Calkins married Harold Finley Beard in 1941 at St. John's Cathedral. The bride's wedding gown of white net and satin complimented her beautiful veil of Venetian rose point lace belonging to Mrs. Perry Hoffman (Mary Louise Corbin.)

For a time newlyweds Mr. and Mrs. J. Malcolm Smith (Mary Louise Calkins) lived at the Norman Ranch. [102]

Ben Norman's original farmhouse was built circa 1883-85, and was known as the Clark's house in 1954. Ben later built a second home here in which Kirtland Cutter added onto in the 1890's, when he erected the cottages along Adar Rd. [103]

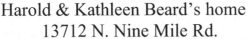

Berg's pic

Harold & Kathleen Beard's home
13712 N. Nine Mile Rd.

Ben's Bungalow
Birchwood aka Norman Ranch

"Birchwood Farm" was the country home of Mr. and Mrs. H. S. Calkins; Miss Harriet Calkins, in the summer months they would entertain the club sisters of the Kappa Chi social club graduates of the Lewis and Clark high school on field trips at "Birchwood Farm." The young socialites continued to return to Birchwood for luncheons on numerous occasions at various events. [104]

In 1952 Harold and Kathleen Beard would later build their own home here adjacent to Ben's bungalow. "Like mother, like daughter, "Kathleen: and her mother Mrs. Harry Simpson Calkins had both worked as treasurer for the Spokane Children's Home and the Ladies Benevolent Society.

Arden Farms was well-known for their ice cream. They delivered fresh dairy products to the Spokane Children's Home and to Birchwood Farm. Later the Beard family had Early Dawn deliver the milk.

BIRCHWOOD FARM aka Norman Ranch was established in 1883, and has been continually owned by the Norman family for more than a Century. But as yet, has never been declared a National Historic Landmark.

It was during the summer months of 1983 when we first met Kathleen during our research at the (MAC) Museum where she was a volunteer. She invited us to see "Birchwood" where she lived nearby her Uncle Bens (deceased) house which sat vacant most of the time. We took a few pictures inside the old farmhouse, when there was no one inside. Later on we show the picture's to certain individuals, their responses varied. While some saw pioneer figures dressed in period clothing 'others' saw nothing at all.

Kathleen Francis Beard was a first-hand source for "Birchwood Farm." She had revealed an oral history of some short stories to the writer's herein. In company with her we remember a few leisurely walks at Birchwood where she lived. On a summer outing in 1988 along with our two young sons Josh and Jason, she told us about some of the farms history that she had committed to memory. That afternoon we shared a picnic lunch with Kathleen next to the Little Spokane River.

 Berg Pic's

Two black walnut trees            Stone remains at Birchwood

What would the two enormous black walnut trees overshadowing the farmhouse say if they could talk? "They'd tell you that life began when Ben planted the little nut trees, after he brought them back from England during his travels in the 1890s."

Located southwest adjacent from the barns were the stone remains of the Birchwood Farm springhouse/ice/cold storage. Before Ben had power he used remnants of a stone wall for food storage into the ground with rock on the hill side.

Early Photo 1890's/courtesy of Kathleen Beard

Ben planted a variety of fruit trees along the Little Spokane River. Located by the barns heading west along the hill side he built a small concrete pond where little jack pines now grow. We leisurely strolled alongside the trail with Kathleen as she pointed out the concrete old pond, now badly cracked with age.

The section of the old rugged trail that runs through Birchwood was known as Adar Lane in 1890. The old stagecoach ran through the Birchwood Farm property aka Norman Ranch nearby the Spokane and the Little Spokane River mouth, now Schumacher Rd - the Cottonwood Rd. then to the town of Colville.

Kathleen liked to tell anecdotes, tales passed down from family members. One humorous tale of times past by Grandpa William was a rat-tale. "On certain occasions Uncle Ben's guests would miss small shiny items. Pocket watches, coins, spoons and forks were nowhere to be found. They finally did catch the pack rat, nothing came up missing after that."

In the company of her husband, she loved riding horse back through the natural trails at Birchwood adjoining the State park.

She remembered, too, when she was a young girl a portrait hung above the fireplace mantel at the "Birchwood Farm Lodge." Uncle Ben was seated with neatly dressed gentlemen. Their demeanor manifests an aristocratic aura—enjoyed privately behind-the scenes, unbeknownst to the public.


## CELEBRATING THE DIAMOND JUBILEE, JUNE 22, 1897

### "The Birchwood Company"
Courtesy of Kathleen Beard /    13 bloodline families + Ben's


Birchwood Farm was incorporated in 1914, an advantage during the Progressive Era; The Origins of the Federal Reserve System, 1897–1913.

Kathleen Frances Beard gave us an oral account and photograph copies of the place where she grew up, and eventually raised her own family at "Birchwood." Mrs. Beard had a genuine passion for the country life. Her character was straightforward.

She could easily bring up fresh stories from the past, relying upon her retentive living memory of "Birchwood." She easily recognized a few faces and names, pointing her finger first in the direction of Uncle Ben, the middleman seated (centre), with other high-ranking Freemasons in a celebratory mood commemorating the Diamond Jubilee at Birchwood.

Most if not all the gentlemen pictured have a rose pinned to their suits. The Latin phrase sub rosa means "under the rose", and is used in English to denote secrecy or confidentiality, similar to the Chatham House Rule. The rose as a symbol of secrecy has an ancient history.

Alex Winston was elected the first Attorney General (1897-1901) for Washington State and in 1889 United States District Attorney in Washington. [105]

Standing behind her Uncle Ben, she recognizes Herbert Bolster the "Father of the Spokane Interstate Fair," and an early W. W. P. incorporator. Standing above Mr. Norman is Mr. Bolster; on his (left) is Thomas Hooker, who 'at the time' was the Spokane Chronicle V-P. Many of these wealthy elite gentlemen and their allied families are connected via bloodlines or intermarriage.

The Spokane Mining Exchange, filed on May 20th 1890 for Articles of Incorporation, and opened its doors for business on July 10, 1890. The management and control of the organization was placed in the hands of thirteen trustees, the board comprised of the following gentlemen; H. W. Augustine, W. H. Taylor, F. E. Goodall, F. R. Moore, L. K. Armstrong, E. J. Brickell, Herbert Bolster, L. C. Dillman, J. C. Fisher, William Wallace, J. W. Chapman, Warren Hussey & A. A. Newberry. Herbert Bolster, Hypotheek Bank Bldg., Spokane, Wash. [106]

In 1890 A. A. Newberry was a charter member and the first president of the Spokane Club in the Columbia building-Lamona Block, adjoining the Spokane Hotel on First Avenue. Among the other Charter members of the Spokane Club were Benjamin Norman, H. B. Nichols, W. H. Taylor, J. L. Prickett, Herbert Bolster, J. W. Chapman, Warren Hussey, Fred Chamberlain, V. C. VanHouten, T. J. Hay, F. R. Moore, H. W. Augustine, T. J. Jefferson and F. Lewis Clark, Lane Gilliam, N. Fred Esign, H. L. Wilson, C. L. Burns and Fred Mason.

The Spokane Stock Exchange continued operating from 1897-1991. In 1892 the Spokane Mining exchange and the Chamber of Commerce occupied rooms within the Hotel Spokane. The exchange solicited new members by private invitation only. Brokers and members affiliated with the Spokane stock exchange privy to "secretive" insider information had a financial advantage, and control to corner the market through the buying and selling of shares and companies stocks, and merchandise.

A similar scenario played out with; Otto and Augustus *Heinze's* in their attempt to corner the stock of United Copper Co. that triggered the Panic of 1907.

The Chamber of Commerce was once known as a Board of Trade before the great fire of 1889.. W. H. Taylor was the president of the Board of Trade and W. S. Norman served three years as secretary.   In the early days of Spokane Mr. Griffith was vice-president, Mr. Newberry was the president and Mr. Reeves was secretary.  Thomas Griffith reserved a room & office in the Spokane Hotel and the Northern Pacific Station situated near-by these offices.  Newberry was one of the heavy stock holders early on in the Hotel Spokane.  In 1884, A. A. Newberry and W. S. Norman sold property for the biggest land owner the Northern Pacific Railroad. [107]

"Since I entered politics, I have chiefly had men's views confided to me privately.  Some of the biggest men in the United States, in the field of commerce and manufacture, are afraid of somebody, are afraid of something.  They know that there is a power somewhere so organized, so subtle, so watchful, so interlocked, so complete, so pervasive, that they had not speak above their breath when they speak in condemnation of it." President Woodrow Wilson - 1913.

Graham Barclay Dennis (1855-1923) was the first life president of the Northwest Mining association in 1894.  He was the organizer and President of the Old Dominion Mine in Stevens County, and a close confidant to B. F. Goodman.

Every year the Northwest Mining Association was formerly opened Monday, Feb 28, at the Hotel Spokane.  One hundred Mining Delegates including the Chairman Sidney Norman of the Pacific Northwest and the surrounding districts would meet at the Spokane Convention in Washington State. [108]

Benjamin Norman has deeply rooted ancestry descending from an old Norman family well-connected in Cheltenham England.  Mr. Norman was a capitalist and upon his early arrival to Spokane Falls Washington

Territory in 1882. He would have been greeted by (family and *friends*) within various Masonic societies.

The Federal Reserve Act was signed / set up by President Woodrow Wilson on December 23, 1913. The Federal Reserve Banks opened for business on November 1914. Ben Norman's Birchwood Farm Company was incorporated on April 29, 1914. Regular meetings were conducted by these men at "the Birchwood Lodge" prominent in business and banking circles, heavily invested in the Mining syndicate, media power, politics, Judges/lawyers, railroad tycoons, well-known hoteliers, real estate, Farm Mortgages, Stock-Exchange, Corporate interests, and by other means.

**The Diamond Jubilee:** was celebrated by the United Kingdom and the rest of the British Empire, as Victoria left Buckingham Palace promptly at 11 a.m. on the morning of June 22, 1897 she pushed a button which transmitted a message by telegraph to the farthest reaches of the British Empire: "From my heart I thank you, my beloved people - May God bless you"

The Company gentlemen in the portrait met in celebration of the Diamond Jubilee, and the ceremonial inauguration of the telegram received from her Majesty the Queen that day during a time at "Birchwood" when the sun was at its highest point of the summer solstice - June 22nd. (The word jubilee comes from the Hebrew word yobel which means "ram's horn trumpet).

These men were among the privileged few who had access to an open line of communication early on. A Telegraph machine was located at Birchwood, while the other one was installed within the Hotel Spokane where Wm. Norman in 1897 was still the company president of the Inland Telephone & Telegraph Company, as well as the co-owner and president of the Hotel Spokane Syndicate, whilst his brother Ben served as the owner and manager of the Hotel. Mr. Norman organized both the Spokane Telephone Co. in which he later sold to the Spokane Telegraph Company where he served as president in 1897. One of W. S. Norman's first endeavors was in 1886 with the territorial Marshall of Washington, C. B. Hopkins. Mr. Hopkins, the editor of "Sunset Telephone Fame" sold three men telephone equipment, including the old remnants of the old government line that ran from Walla Walla, Washington to Missoula. William "Billy" Norman together with three partners S. Z. Michell, Lieutenant Fred Sparling and Burt Nichols organized Spokane's first telephone Company. The Northern Pacific and the Court House were customers early on. Mr. Norman later paid off his business partners. In 1888 Charles B. Hopkins and William Norman organized the Inland Telephone and Electric Company. "The Company began the Bell Telephone system – as the two were licensed with the American Bell Telephone (Alexander Graham Bell).

W. S. Norman held a monopoly from 1887-1889 with the line running through to the Coeur d'Alene's from Spokane. Mr. Norman put patents on: The Spokane Falls and Wardner Telephone-Telegraph Lines, W. S. Norman, owner, Spokane Falls, Wash. Received and filed on August 17, 1887 with the (postal laws & regulations of the U. S. of America) W. S. Norman's U. S. Military Telegraph Line. Between Fort Coeur d'Alene and Spokane Falls, Wash. Received and filed October 13, 1887. Mr. Norman informed Nelson Wayne Durham that "The Bell Company" operated for several years under the name of the Inland Company, and subsequently changed to the Pacific States." In 1890 Wm. Norman sold his interest to the Inland Telephone & Telegraph Co., remained as president until 1897. Levi Hutton was one of W. S. Norman's linemen in the early years kept the lines in order at the summit on the top of Fourth of July canyon aided by a pony. Mr. Hutton later with his wife May "the suffragette" made a fortune in the North Idaho, Hercules Mine, and built the Hutton building and the Hutton Settlement. In 1889 a great fire engulfed the thirty-two block business district of Spokane. Subsequently that same year Washington would become a state in November 1889. [109]

Ben enjoyed his summer home at "Birchwood Farm." His chain of hotels; afforded him a comfortable and luxurious lifestyle. When he arrived at the Spokane Hotel he relaxed in his own private suite #228. On occasion Ben would entertain "Ernestine Schumann-Heink (1861-1936) an operatic contralto at Birchwood." Two impresarios, Miss Lois Steers and Mrs. Frederick Schram (Wynn Coman), both of Portland, spent part of every summer at Birchwood for twenty-seven years. [110]

The Great Seattle Fire on June 6th 1889, consumed **32** city blocks. Then just two months later the big Spokane fire broke out on August 4th 1889, wreaking havoc in its wake and destroyed **32** city blocks – including most of the hotels in its path.

As luck would have it – the Hotel Spokane and Washington Water Power buildings were two of the Norman bros. The flames spared the original five-story brick building located on the Boston Block business district at 521 W. 1st Avenue and Stevens St., Spokane, WA. The Boston Block Building was initially built by B. F. Burch and Henry Brooks and was used for an office building, warehouse and hotel, located at the Hotel Spokane Block - home to the Mining Exchange.

In the early 1880's the Brooks family lived on the future site of the Hotel Spokane.

Dr. Benjamin Burch mingled with the early 'moneymen' of Spokane where he owned extensive property.

After the fire, lodging was desperately needed. Lucky for Ben Norman he came prepared with his own tent, as he was the owner of the Spokane Tent Company early on in 1884-85. Spokane citizens longed for a Hotel fashioned to provide both business and pleasure for customers in and outside of town. The Spokane Hotel had been built up from the original five story brick building to six stories.

In 1889 Herman Preusse an early Spokane architect transformed the warehouse interior into a luxurious Hotel. Mr. Preusse designed more buildings after the great fire than any other architect. Hardly any of his commercial buildings are left standing today, that includes the Spokane Hotel. The Spokane Club began in the Lamona Building.

The Norman brothers purchased the Hotel Spokane and the Lamona Building from the Northwest Pacific Hypotheek Bank for $80,000 and joined the two buildings together.

David B. Fotheringham (1st mayor of Spokane) was one of the builder's who erected the Hotel Spokane and other notable buildings. Mr. Fotheringham was vice-pres of the Washington Brick, Lime &

Manufacturing Company that Henry Brook organized.  An ambiance of "old world English Charm" surrounded the Hotel. [111]

Hotel Spokane picture - Author's Collection

The Norman brothers opened their doors to the Spokane, fashioned with white cylindrical columns, pillars beautify the Hotel lobby.  The Norman brothers were unwavering "pillars of the community", not to mention indispensible to the Hotel Syndicate in their attempt to continue operating the Hotel during the 1893 panic.

Wm. Norman pleaded to his creditors of the Spokane Hotel syndicate, as well as the W.W.P.  A 'tone of irony' here, the W.W.P corridors of 'power' began on March 13th 1889 with Wm. Norman, an early promoter and secy/manager – along with nine other Power players. One of which, included his brother in law, Frank Rockwood Moore, the company's first pres.  The big fire never reached the W.W.P. building. [112]

The Federal Reserve is the central banking system of the United States. It was created on December 23, 1913, with the enactment of the Federal Reserve Act to avert upcoming bank panics; in response to a series of financial panics (particularly the panic of 1907.)  The 1893 panic was a serious economic depression in the U. S. an extension of the panic of 1873. That same year 73 the Father of Spokane (J. N. Glover), Ide and Goodman arrived to the Wash. Territory. The depression ended in 1897.

James Breen and Herman Bellinger, both metallurgists' quit Heinze to join the new Le Roi Mining and Smelting Co, registered in B. C. on August, 1897. [113]

In 1899 the Norman Hotel Co., took in their *friend* and partner James Breen, the well-known smelting operator of Northport, Wash., in cooperation with the Le Roi Northport Smelter. The Norman brothers in 1900 together with James refashioned the Spokane Hotel distinguishing it as a famous hotel of the Inland Empire. The Spokane Hotel Co., profited as a result of the gold rush in Rossland B.C. Later on the Syndicate membership included a $200.000 investment in the Hotel by three heavy stock holders, William Norman, James Breen and John Dickenson Sherwood. Ben and W. S. Norman took over the interest of James Breen in the Spokane and Tacoma Hotel companies, purchasing about one third of capital stock. [114]

In 1905 the Norman brothers and Mr. Breen purchased the Tacoma Hotel and hired K. K. Cutter to remodel the hotel. William Blackwell as business secretary kept financial interest in the Tacoma Hotel Co. Blackwell was a thirty-second degree mason of the Scottish rite and the El Katif Temple of the Mystic Shrine and a member of other fraternities. The back balcony of the hotel revealed the beautiful bay as guests watched the ships sail by.

James Breen and Con Hayes purchased the Gregson resort in 1901 from the Gregson brothers George and Ely. Miners and smelter men from nearby Butte and Anaconda were regular customers of the hotel. See Also; Hayes-Monnette lease, 1906, Goldfield, Nevada 863 / The Famous Mohawk Mine? Another interesting note; the giant reef mining co. crescent Nevada, was the Normans mine.

C. A. Broadwater built the Broadwater Hotel in 1889. Charles in 1892 Mr. Broadwater's nephew, Thomas A. Marlow, controlled the Broadwater. The hotel closed in 1894 until James Breen re-opened the Broadwater on January 4th 1907. James Breen was a partner of the Norman brothers in hotels & mining. He was also connected with the Copper King trio, William Andrews Clark, Marcus Daly and Augustus

Fritz Heinze of Butte, Montana. Hugh Daly was the proprietor of Gregson Hot Springs present day Fairmont Hot Springs purchased the Broadwater Hotel back from Breen in 1916.

Benjamin Norman connected with Granger families, and husbandry; that said; he controls the Palouse through the banks. Mr. Oliver Wilson was the Worthy Master, of the National Grange located in Spokane, Wash; in which a Telegram was received and appreciated, "Warmest Greeting to officers and members of the National Grange." The Secretary presented a communication signed by the Chamber of Commerce of Spokane and the master of Washington State Grange, guaranteeing hotel rates on hall accommodations which were satisfactory to the committee. "It is interesting to note here; that Scott and Janet Wolter, theorize a connection of the granger families, and husbandry to the Venus families." [115]

Ex-attorney General Monnet, of the Ohio National Grange was instrumental in passing the Sherman Antitrust Act of 1890. [116]

In 1890 Elizabeth O'GRADY married Marcus O'FARRELL the nephew of the 'Copper King' Marcus Daly who was the president of the Anaconda Copper mine in Montana. Elizabeth 'some time later' became a widow and went on to marry James Breen. He was known widely for his expertise in examining mining claims, and smelting ore. The actions of the Heinze brothers had caused much of the panic/Knickerbocker Crisis in the 1907 crash that eventually lead to the formation of the US Federal Reserve System in 1913-14 the same time, the Birchwood Farm Company incorporated. James Breen was a partner of the BFC, the Hotel Spokane Syndicate, and a partner in 1907 with the "copper king" F. Augustus Heinz "Broadwater Hotel."

The United Copper Company operated for only a short time. The organization was incorporated in 1902 by F. Augustus Heinze (1869–1914), the same company that played a key part in the panic, as a result of the 1907 depression. Heinze instilled trepidation and "the public panicked and stampeded for the banks." The Heinze "bros" (like the ancient God Pan) were the perpetrators who caused much of the Bankers' pan-ic in the 1907 economic crash. J. Pierpont Morgan financed several trust companies from insolvency, and rescued the New York Stock Exchange.

During our research we came across the Rev. Jonathan Edward's (book History of Spokane County 1900) herein; a descendent from the theologian and minister Jonathan Edwards (1703-1758), a 1720 graduate of Yale College, whose namesake is the Jonathan Edwards College a residential college at Yale University in New Haven, Connecticut, (Skull & Bones). One of his maternal ancestors was James *Pierpont*, a founder of Yale, whose daughter married *Jonathan Edwards*. [117]

In 1910, Heinze married Bernice Henderson, an actress who played the role of a vampire on stage. After the two married a son was born, Fritz Augustus Heinze, Jr., his parents divorced two years later. The United Copper Company of Montana was formed in 1902, to take over the properties of Heinze and his associates. James Walton was the superintendent for the United Copper Co. He is recognized as a man of great knowledge and experience in mining, doing much development work on the above properties during the coming season. Mr. Walton some time ago secured a smelter site for this company, which can not be equaled in this section. The facts contradict Jonathan Edwards, that James is not ambitious for leadership qualities. [118]

The panic/depression of 1893 caused widespread apprehension, joblessness, lowering copper prices, as a result mining and smelting activity slowed. Hundreds of mines closed in and outside the U. S. That same year the Spokane Hotel Company went bankrupt, and requested assistance from their mtg. co., the Northwestern & Pacific Hypotheek Bank. In 1894 rather than see the hotel close the NW&PH (Binkley) mortgage company allowed the Norman brothers to pay on the hotel at virtually no cost for the first six months and then for two years at five hundred dollars ($500.) per month.

It was imperative the Hotel Spokane not close due to bankruptcy. The hotel was the heart of the business center for the entire communities in and outside the town. Sidney Norman had stated that the Hotel Spokane was the real mining center of the Northwest. Spokane was the designated headquarters for the North Idaho mines, as well as the

Business center for the Inland Empire. In 1889 the Hotel Spokane was the power base for the Mining Exchange in the Pacific Northwest.

The firm Binkley & Taylor (Montvale Farm) managed the NW&PH Bank until 1896. During the early years the hotel cashier was Herbert Moore. Herbert was a relative of Fred Mason and Frank Moore (Spokane Mayor for two years 1907-09), and secy. of the Spokane Street Railway/ Spokane Cable Railway and business associate of Finch and Campbell. [119]

Frank Rockwood Moore passed away in 1895. Ben Norman, Charles Sweeny, J. D. Sherwood, James N. Glover, the "founding father" of Spokane, Henry Brook and Deputy Sheriff Lane C. Gilliam were his pallbearers at the funeral. Ben Norman was dressed in a white suit. A wake was held at "Birchwood," for close friends and relatives. A few of the gentlemen in *attendance*, were; W. S. Norman, and his wife Aimee (Sherlock) Norman, her sister, Sarah Francis "Fanny" (Sherlock), and Frank's mother in-law, Rosetta Sherlock. The three (Sherlock) ladies were finely dressed in black. Sidney Norman, the nephew of Frank was also present, as well as Herbert Bolster. [120]

However, W. S. Norman sagaciously reorganized the Spokane Hotel stock and remodeled the hotel. The Normans Hotel business revived and continued successfully following the Le-Roi Mine discovery. Spokane and the nearby communities rapidly increased in population with the Railroad and mining boom. Ben Norman received the title to the Spokane Hotel in 1895. [121]

Concurrently, the American Mining Company of James Walton, failed the property was leased by the Northwest Copper Company in 1896-97. In 1898 the Northwest Copper Company built a smelter at Cuprum, Idaho to handle the ore from the Peacock Mine, Seven Devils District Hells Canyon.

The Edison Illuminating Company was established in 1880 by Thomas Edison. Electrical generating stations were initially constructed throughout New York City. The company was the prototype for other local illuminating companies that were established in the United States during the 1880s.  W. S. Norman in 1887 helped promote the Edison Electric Illuminating Co., organized under the laws of the State of Washington on April 18, 1888.  S. Z. Mitchell and Fred Sparling were N.W. agents for the electric Co. operating under the Edison license. Mitchell and Sparling engineered and operated a crane elevator, run by a 15 horsepower Thomson-Houston motor in the Hotel Spokane.  In 1892 Thomson-Houston merged with the Edison companies forming the giant General Electric Co. [122]

From the Spokane Daily Chronicle, Newspaper Accounts; eight men were arrested for violating the midnight closing ordinance, No, A 900:  The following names appeared on the police station register, December 19-1899.  J.H. Wilmot, saloonkeeper, William F. McClurg, bartender, T.H. Tollefson, saloonkeeper, Roy R. Rorman, bartender, B. Norman, hotelkeeper, L.M. Davenport, restaurant keeper, William Watson, hotelkeeper/Pedicord Hotel, G.F. Algeo bartender.  The Spokane Hotel and the Davenport restaurant were both involved in the violation of the new midnight ordinance.  They did not deny that they were selling liquor.  According to the hotel men, their Attorney Richard Watson "Dick" Nuzum, a (French Huguenot) advised the saloon men not to close their saloons, "implying that the innkeeper's will repeat the offense in the future".

The Silver Grill restaurant opened in 1903 on the second floor adjacent the charming dining room in the Hotel Spokane.  K. K. Cutter, Spokane's famous architect (began his career/1889) designed the Silver Grill for the Normans.  The Norman Hotel Ltd. parked tour cars out front for guests during their stay at the Hotel Spokane, Tacoma Hotel, North Yakima Hotel, and the Portland Hotel, where visitor's were picked up and taken to the Railroad stations.  Sightseers in Spokane would tour the Manito Park area, Browne's Addition, Liberty Lake, Waikiki, and other neighborhoods.  Parlors on the second floor entertained guests with luxurious furnishings, separate bathrooms and closets on every floor.  The immaculate accommodations assured satisfied guests of a charming atmosphere.  In earlier times, from coast to coast the famous "Silver Grill" entertained and housed regular customers including famous celebrities, world-renowned dignitaries and Politician's.  The Silver Grill was reminiscent of an Old English Inn Room in America. [123]

Hotel Spokane / Berg's photo (Libby)

President Theodore Roosevelt including Washington State representatives since the Progressive Era enjoyed "The Spokane's" famous hotel hospitality. Teddy was a distant cousin to FDR both presidents were high level freemasons. Theodore Roosevelt the first president to visit Spokane in 1903 stayed at the Hotel Spokane. On May 26, 1903, he broke ground for a Spokane Masonic Temple. Teddy Roosevelt and Pres. Herbert Hoover a "Boho" (Bohemian Grove) and his sons including Thomas E. Dewey were served by Clarence Taylor who manned the well-known "Silver Traveling Cart". William Jennings Bryan said "the roast beef and the prime ribs served by Clarence were the best he ever ate".

President Arthur "tapped" George Turner to the Washington Territory Supreme Court in 1884. Turner had a financial interest in the Le Roi mine and was a member of the Scottish Rite Masons, the El Katif Shrine, the Spokane Lodge No. 34 in 1885 and the Royal Arch Mason in Spokane in 1932. Turner was a member of the territorial convention in 1889 that framed the first state constitution of Washington. The Corbin and Moore-Turner Heritage Gardens established in 1889. Roosevelt returned to Spokane many times, often visiting with Senator George Turner who served Washington in the U. S. Senate (1896-1902). [124]

The Norman brothers were formerly from England; exceptional British "mine hosts" creating an awe inspiring ambiance of their great fireplace and grill.

## Above the fireplace "hung the sign" with the catchy phrase;

He may live without Books ~ what is knowledge but grieving? He may live without hope ~ what is hope but deceiving?  He may live without love ~ what is passion but pinning?  But where is the Man that ~ can live without Dining? [125]

William Norman's idea for the traveling silver cart was inspired by a similar model noted during his stay at Simpson's, the strand in London. In 1898 Wm. bought the original cart in Paris from Christofle, a world famous silversmith for 3200 francs.

Clarence L. Taylor in 1902 began operating the silver cart at 12 years of age.  He was a handsome young African American boy standing by to baste the meat in the fireplace grill.  Next to its fireplace, with its spit, guests watched meat as it spun on a crane while roasting.  The silver traveling cart was wheeled to the guests table where the meat was carved. Considered a masterpiece the original 1898 Christofle cart was copied in this country by Gorham and Reed and Barton, who sent craftsmen to Spokane to see it.  The top of the cart glowed like a luminescent orb.

Customers preferring the regular cuisine of the hotel relaxed in the attractive dining room or chose the traveling silver carte method performed in the Silver Grill.  Banquet rooms were readily available for parties or receptions.  The meeting room of the hotel held Spokane civic groups and service clubs. In 1899 Colonel William M. Ridpath built the Ridpath Hotel in Spokane Washington.

Mr. Ridpath's daughter Mary married John D. Ankeny on July 18, 1906. W. M. Ridpath made a huge fortune along with the Norman brothers, James Breen and others investor's of the famous Le Roi mine. Clarence Taylor and the Silver serving traveling cart both moved to the Ridpath Hotel in 1961 when the new hotel was built. In 1963 a new modern motel was built across from the Ridpath to take the place of the Hotel Spokane. The Silver Grill was remodeled inside the Ridpath, Ankeny's Restaurant is located on the top floor. The Ridpath Hotel has bankrupted, suffering the same fate as the Hotel Spokane. But, the Hotel Spokane recovered and profited, as a result of the mining industry in Spokane. Fish, turtles and plants inhabited the pond in the Silver Grill, Hotel Spokane. [126]

**The Silver Grill Nuggets**…1930's…Berg's picture
Entertainers performing in the Silver Grill

Al Marineau & his Silver Grill Nuggets would often entertain at the Hotel Spokane Silver Grill. Albert Alexander Marineau was born in 1902 - 1984. Albert *Alexander Marineau* of Coeur d'Alene had been elected Student Director of the University of *Idaho Pep Band* for a number of years.

Nearby Farms and merchants included Birchwood and Montvale Farms, supplied the Hotel with fresh fruits, vegetables, meats and dairy. Judge Binkley grew "Spokane Beauty apples" especially for the Spokane Hotel at his Montvale Farm. [127]

The renowned Silver Grill Apple Pie Recipe as follows; Core, peel and slice enough fresh, tart, well-washed apples to give six cups of apple slices about ¼ -inch thick. Place apple slices in bowl and dredge them with a mixture of 1/3 cup sugar, ½ teaspoon cinnamon and a pinch of nutmeg. Combine all the peelings and cores with 1 pint water, ½ cup honey, ½ cup sugar and two teaspoons lemon juice. Simmer gently for about ½ hour. Strain off liquid and thicken it with 1 ½ level teaspoons cornstarch dissolved in a little cold water. This liquid is to be added to the pie after it is baked. Line a 9-inch pie pan with good flaky-type pastry rolled to about the thickness of a nickel. Pile sliced and sugared apples lightly into shell; cover with a pastry top into which has been cut ½ inch circular vent to allow for escape of steam. Brush top crust with milk to aid browning. Bake in preheated 400 degree oven for 30 min. Remove pie from oven pour into it through the top vent as much of the liquid mixture as the pie will hold. Let pie cool to room temperature before cutting. [128]

## Chapter 16
### The Norman Bros. Chain of Hotels

The Yakima Hotel initially opened for business on July 4, 1889. Ben and his brother William Norman together with James Breen leased the North Yakima Hotel Company on June 1st 1907. The three hotel men were well-known for successfully operating a chain of hotels in the West under the surname of the Norman Hotels, Ltd. The Yakima Hotel situated at 3rd. Street and Yakima Avenue was conveniently located close by the Northern Pacific Railroad. The Yakima trolleys running more than a century ago still operate today. The Norman Hotels, Ltd. including Mr. Breen in 1910 associated themselves with the Portland Hotel proprietors in Multnomah, Oregon. The Norman brothers and James Breen owned stock in the Portland Hotel together along with the Day brothers, Eugene, Jerome and Harry Day, these partners were a coterie of capitalists in lucrative mining endeavors as well. Edward Boyce (1862-1941) was a heavy stockholder and the Portland Hotel Company President. Charles E. Leland was the first manager of the Portland Hotel. The Leland's are well-known hoteliers of Albany, Saratoga, Brighton Beach and other famous hotels. [129]

In 1911 H. C. Bowers became the President and manager of the Bowers Hotel (formerly known as the Nortonia Hotel), located in Portland, Oregon. Mr. Bowers had once managed the famous Arlington Hotel, "the Spokane" and later "the Portland" for 17 years, as well as a stockholder of the Portland Hotel Co. The Hotel Multnomah opened on February 1st, 1912. H. C. Bowers moved to the Multnomah Hotel in 1914, and the name of the Bowers Hotel changed back to Nortonia. The Nortonia is presently known as the Mark Spencer Hotel. See Philip Spencer-mutiny.

The Davenport Hotel located in Spokane, Washington began construction in 1913, designed by Kirkland Kelsey Cutter (1860-1939) and Karl Malmgren. Louis M. Davenport (1868-1951) a restaurateur opened the Grand Hotel for business on September 1, 1914. One hundred stock holders invested the money to build the Davenport Hotel at a cost of nearly two million dollars. One of the investor's included, F. Lewis Clark, of Spokane, who sold the land and carried the contract for Louis Davenport to help build his Davenport Hotel. [130]

Mr. Davenport owned a 440-acre summer estate named Flower field, located on the Little Spokane River, Nine Mile Falls, Washington. Neighboring farms integrated Davenport's Flower field, Binkley's Montvale, Grave's Waikiki Dairy, Griffith's Glen Tana Dairy and Birchwood Farm are all down river from the Spokane fish hatchery. Saint George's School was established in 1955 as St. George's Episcopal School, purchasing 120 acres of Flower field. L.M. Davenport, Ben Norman, W.S. Norman, J.W. Binkley, Jay P. Graves and Thomas S. Griffith, were close friends and business associates who graciously entertained one another at their Spokane stately manors or country estates. The Spokane Country Club was conveniently located nearby these gentlemen ranches. The Glen Tana horse races were by private invitation only on private property – closed off to all 'outsiders'.

Later the Davenport remained closed through 1985-2000. Civic and community leaders worked to save the hotel from demolition. Walt and Karen Worthy purchased the hotel and re-opened her in 2002.

James Breen passed away in Butte, Montana at the age of 62 on 8-11-1925. That same year the Norman bros. sold some of their hotel co., interest to John E. Savage (Butler Hotel) in Puget Sound, in spite of that the Norman's remained actively involved in numerous mining activities.

Ben Norman remained a bachelor and resided at the Hotel Spokane, where he later passed away at 84 years of age, on February 17, 1934. His brother William later inherited the Birchwood Farm Estate.

Ben Norman was born 1849 in England, where he later attended the Cheltenham Grammar School. Afterward he occupied as a "coal merchant" in Bays Hill, Cheltenham, during his residence in the Alpha House/Jenner House (now a museum), with his family.

His cousins were the Cummings whom the Norman's had adopted. William Cummings converged with the Norman brothers early on in Spokane, Washington. Mr. Cummings owned property in Nine Mile Falls, Washington early on. Ben Norman's great niece, Kathleen Beard remembered the story of the Devil's Chimney-at present a local landmark could be viewed from the Norman's home in London. She told us interesting stories about her Grandpa William Norman and his cousin William Cummings. The young boys would climb to the top of Devil's chimney, to gather baby ravens, to train and keep as pets. A more scientific derivation of the rock's origin is offered by the 19th Century geologist S. Buckman, brother-in-law to Benjamin Norman; Darwinian; The Devil's Chimney in Cheltenham resembles that of the Devils Gulch in South Dakota, where Frank Goodman was robbed by bandits.)

Edward Jenner lived in his Cheltenham summerhouse in 1800 on High St; and he later resided at 8, St. Georges Street here spanning the years 1802-1813. Mr. Jenner was vaccinating gratuitously at Alpha House. Later Bayshill became the residence of George Norman mayor of Cheltenham. Two manifestos which spans 1606-1**616** were published in Germany and Europe - the Rosicrucian *Fama Fraternitis RC*, and the

Confessio Fraternitatis. In 1795 Dr. Edward Jenner (1749-1823) was a
pioneer scientist, Rosicrucian, notable freemason, FRS in 1788 (Fellow of
the Royal Society), and (Order of the Rosy Cross.) He is best-known as
the "Father of Immunology." He was a British scientist and a naturalist
who was educated by *John Hunter.*

Dr. Jenner occupied the Alpha House, Bayshill, St George's Place,
Cheltenham, United Kingdom for the purpose of charity/gratuitous
vaccination in 1795. The Ancient and Mystical Order Rosæ Crucis
(AMORC), also calls itself the Rosicrucian Order. Rosicrucianism is a
philosophical secret society said to have been founded in late medieval
Germany by Christian Rosenkreuz. It holds a doctrine or theology "built
on esoteric truths of the ancient past," which are "concealed from the
average man, provide insight into nature, the physical universe and the
spiritual realm."

Rosicrucianism is symbolized by the Rosy Cross or Rose Cross. Edward
Jenner was elected FRS on 26 February 1789; initiated in Lodge of Faith
and Friendship No. 449, Gloucestershire. Between the years 1607 and
1616, two anonymous manifestos were published, first in Germany and
later throughout Europe. These were the Fama Fraternitatis RC (The
Fame of the Brotherhood of RC) and the Confessio Fraternitatis (The
Confession of the Brotherhood of RC).

The influence of these documents, presenting a "most laudable Order" of
mystic-philosopher-doctors and promoting a "Universal Reformation of
Mankind", gave rise to an enthusiasm called by its historian Dame
Frances Yates the "Rosicrucian Enlightenment". Everything is linked.
The Georgia Guide stones are no exception; where a man named R. C.
Christian, a Rosicrucian commissioned the monument. [131]

Benjamin is the son of George and Honore (Thomas) Norman.
George Norman Senior was the publisher and proprietor of numerous
newspaper companies in Cheltenham England. George Norman Sr.,
George Curtis Rowe and James Boodle are the original proprietors of the
Cheltenham Examiner in which the Office of the Gloucestershire Bank
adjoined the building. [132]

Ben Norman's older brother, George Norman Jr. was born in 1842 Cheltenham England where in later years he served as Alderman Mayor (1898-1901). George Jr. was an editor/stationer of the firm Norman, Sawyer & Company in Cheltenham England. Brother George Norman was a Past Master, Quatuor Coronati Lodge No. 2076 in London and a founder of The Organon Lodge No. 3,233 w/ (Homeopathy.)

George Norman Jr. and Emma Mary (Boodle) Norman are the parents of Sidney Norman. Dr. George Norman of Bath, Quatuor Coronati Lodge 2076, Brother Norman was a Past Asst Grand Dir, Senior Deacon of the Masonic ceremonies.

The Mayor and Commonalty and Citizens of the City of London Corporation, is the municipal governing body of the City of London, the historic centre of London and the location of most of the UK's financial sector. The corporate structure includes the Lord Mayor, the Court of Aldermen, the Court of Common Council, and the Freemen and Livery of the City.

Ben Norman was an ironmonger. The Ironmongers aka *Ferroners*, were incorporated under a Royal Charter in 1463. Ironmongers' Hall is the home of the "Worshipful Company of Ironmongers" is one of the livery companies of the City of London located in Aldersgate St. City of London. [133]

## Chapter 17
## "Ripperology" - 1888

We ourselves are not "ripperologists," but genuinely interested in the facts--referring to the mood of a series of murders that took place in London in 1888. The killer/killer's have never been identified, getting away scot-free *right under the noses* of the City of *London Police*. The slayer/slayer's dubbed "Jack the Ripper," of Scotland Yard remains a mystery. The Ripper stories are rife with *Masonic-mystery*.

Stranger still *our story* is replete with "ripperology", and high-level masons-members within the *Lodge 2076*, who have been frequently implicated by authors -relative to the "Jack the Ripper" theories. Brother George Norman was a founding member of Lodges, in 1886 under the jurisdiction of the United Grand Lodge of England. George Norman contributed a vast number of papers when he was the second Past Worshipful Master of *Quatuor Coronati Lodge No. 2076*" - the oldest Research Lodge in London" a particular type of *Masonic lodge* dutiful to Masonic research, as a lodge, and as such has a charter from some *Grand Lodge*. It accepts members from all over the world through its Correspondence Circle. A book of transactions called *Ars Quatuor Coronatorum* (which includes the papers given in the lodge) has been published every year since 1886. [134]

Rober Freke *Gould* contributed twenty-five papers and many notes to Ars Quatuor Coronatorum spanning 1836–1915. By chance, could R. F. *Gould* be related to the (*Gould*/Strickland bloodlines) mentioned herein? Sir Charles Warren had insider knowledge to study the craft, and was an authority on Freemasonic history and ritual. He was an English archaeologist, Surveyor of Herod's Temple, Royal Lodge of *Friendship* No. 278 Gibraltar. General Sir Charles Warren GCMG, KCB, FRS (1840–1927) was an officer in the British Royal Engineers. He was one of the early European archaeologists of the Biblical Holy Land, and the Temple Mount/New Jerusalem. Bro. Charles Warren was a Police Commissioner of London (1886-1888) during a period of unrest, as a result of the "Jack the Ripper" multiple murders. [135]

Charles Warren, P. M. Past Master in 1862, worked on the survey of Gibraltar from 1861-65, and was an officer in the Royal Engineers and then Police Commissioner of the Metropolis *concurrent* with the Ripper murders. In 1867 he unearthed a "water shaft" aka "Warren's shaft during the time of the *first* major excavation of Jerusalem, and a series of tunnels underneath the Temple Mount. Albert Edward, Prince of Wales, G.M., (Grand Master) No. 2076 Lodge. [136]

A *clue* to the killer/killer's identity could be his nickname, "Jack-the-ripper." One might study the symbols and legends behind the Scythe, Ripper/Reaper. Another factor to consider in the Ripper murders is the principles of sacred geometry, numerology, astronomy, geometry, to name a few.  Lastly and more importantly, Biblical prophecies and theology, (revelation reveals truth and or knowledge).

Biblical verse; (Joel 2:24) Revelation 14:14-19  "The Two Reapers" a sharp sickle (Rev. 14:14 – 20:9-10)  Clusters of grapes from the earth's *vine* because its grapes are ripe - Take your sharp sickle and gather the harvest.  And still another Angel came out from the altar; their wickedness is great.  The vats are full.  5th seal – the harvest has come.  Daughter of Babylon – "threshing barn" - The harvest of the earth - The rapture of the church - sharp sickle.  **7** angels – **7** plagues – **7** Devils (Rev. 15.6)

"Burke and Hare" were 18th Century surgeons, amid John Hunter, and Edward Jenner of the Royal Navy.  Due to a shortage of bodies, allegedly body snatchers were buying corpses for medical study. [137]

George Norman (1783-1861) lived at 1 Circus Bath, a fellow of the Royal College of Surgeons.  The royal society shareholders in the (EIC) EAST INDIA COMPANY - (Dutch) took the minerals deposits. [138]

See; the trio of Goodman's Fields Theatres situated nearby *Whitechapel* in the *East End* of London, and Aldergate East Underground stations by which the killer may have gone through as a "traveling man" seemingly unnoticed, from west to the east-end.

The study of the Craft degrees is replete with masonic ritual, the way the Ripper killed his victim's, see; "penal sign", and the three "Juwes," Jubela, Jubelo and Jubelum.

– "Note Worthy" Diana, Princess of Wales 'Frances, nee Spencer' died by accident on AUG 31st 1997, the date of the "Ripper's first murder victim" AUG 31st 1888.
See; Oedipus / Divinity / Necromancy, lust killings, and Black magic sacrifice-entrails.

Sherlock Holmes quoted from the story series - Sir Arthur Conan Doyle; "How often have I said to you, that when you have eliminated the impossible, whatever remains, however improbable, must be the truth?"

## Chapter 18
## Sidney Norman moves to Spokane Falls – 1889

Sidney Norman (1870-1956) left England and moved to Spokane Falls, W.T., arriving in time for his Uncle William and Aimee L. Sherlock's marriage. His aunt and uncle were married on April 25th 1889. William and Amy Norman resided in a mansion once located at West 644 7th Ave., situated straight across the street from Aimee's sister Sarah & Frank Rockwood Moore's mansion. Sidney Norman would later marry Maria Ellis Winston (1876-1969) ten years later. Maria's childhood memories are "filled in" with a gracious back-story amongst her siblings inside "Windsor Castle," a plantation at Windsor, N. C. To them Virginia Winston Norman (1902-1972), & Winston Norman (1907-1974) & Frank Winston Norman (1918-2006) were born. [139]

Maria Winston Norman (1876-1965) is the daughter of Col. Patrick Henry Winston (1847-1904) and Virginia Beeson Miller (1851-1934) who wedded in 1870. (The Winston's arrived in the midst - along with the other First Families of Virginia).

Patrick Henry Winston - "Give Me Liberty, Or Give Me Death!" Patrick Henry Winston was born on Aug. 22, 1847, and is related to the Prime Minister of the U. K. Sir Winston Churchill / 11th cousin 6 times removed. Randolph Henry Spencer Churchill is the father of British Prime Minister, (Winston Churchill). Patrick Henry Winston Jr. (1820-1886) arrived to Spokane in 1884. P. H. Winston Jr. owned/ edited The Albemarle Times published in Windsor, N. C., and the Spokane Review and Winston's Weekly in Spokane. Patrick Henry Winston died in the Hotel Spokane on April 3rd. 1904. He is buried in the Greenwood Cemetery in Spokane. [140]

Alexander Miller Winston (1872-1936) was Ben Norman's in-law and personal Attorney. Ben named Alex Winston and W. S. Norman as executors of his estate. The Winston brothers are best-known as pioneer lawyers, publishers and politicians. Alexander Winston entered the University of N.C. in 1891 initiated into the Sigma Alpha Epsilon fraternity. [141]

Lt. Gov. Francis Donnell Winston (1857-1941) is clearly identifiable, having served two years as Grandmaster in North Carolina.

George Tayloe Winston (1852-1932) is well-documented and 'at one time,' was the president of the University of N.C. [142]

During Prohibition in Washington State William Norman was arrested- for bootlegging, in1916 Barrels and Cases of whiskey were found hidden in the Hotel Spokane basement in secret rooms and passages used to carry the hidden liquor. [143]

Aimee L. Norman was born in 1865 she predeceased her husband, passing away December 29, 1948 in their luxurious home. [144]

William Sheppard Norman reserved business offices in the Hotel Spokane for his extensive mining interest until his passing August 12, 1954.  The Norman mine was located 6 mi. S. E. of Northport Wash., of which Sidney Norman was SEC/TREAS/MGR/V.P. of the Norman Mines Co.

William and Ben Norman had exclusive mining claims from Mexico to Alaska and were heavy shareholders in the Los Lugos Gold Mining Company, Zacatecas, Guadalajara, Mexico; A Washington Corp. The Giant Reef Mining Co. incorporated in Spokane and was as located in Crescent, Nev., and Trustees: were the Norman bros. of Spokane, the Polson bros. of Hoquiam & others. [145]

Sidney Norman had a private room #201 within the Hotel Spokane. He stayed there on November 29, 1920, 'at that time,' he was the supervisor of the Hotel.  Mr. Sidney Norman of Los Angeles California was a former Spokane resident.  He was once occupied as the Managing Editor, of the Northwest Mining Truth.  The Mining Truth Publishing Co. was located within the Mohawk Building in Spokane.  The Norman Mining Company organized in 1915.  Sidney was the mining editor of the Vancouver Daily Sun., located in B.C. Canada.

## Chapter 19
## The Northport Smelter aka Le Roi Smelter

In 1890 a Spokane Syndicate bought the claim called the Le Roi Co. for $30.000. The Syndicate managed the Northport Smelter from the early 1890's – 98. They in turn sold to the American British Corp. for three million. Initially in 1895 the ore had been shipped to the Heinze trail smelter until the "Company" built its own smelter at Northport, Wash. in 1898. One year later Mr. Breen together with his partners the Norman brothers bought the smelter. Later the partners purchased the adjoining land and buildings from John A. Finch. Harry Day bought the Northport Smelter in 1915 from James Breen and his associates. [146]

Frederick Hamilton Mason visited Spokane in 1883 after investing in real estate he moved here three years later. Mr. Mason was occupied in the hardware business, and opened the Holley Mason Co. in 1888. Fred Mason was the brother of Frank Rockwood Moore who 'at one time' was the V.P. and treas. of the Holley Mason Hardware Co. F. H. Mason was a pioneer charter member of the Spokane Club and Co. Pres. 1900-02. C. Herbert Moore was one of the original stockholders of the Holley-Mason Hardware Co. The Northport Smelter ordered parts for the equip. maintenance from the Company. [147]

In 1913 Francis John Finucane (1901-1984), was the pres. of the Holley-Mason Hardware until Marshall-Wells Hardware took over the Company. His brother Charles C. Finucane (1905-1983) was a co-owner and once president of the Davenport Hotel (1947-1953). Lt. Charles Sweeny (1849-1916) was a hero of the French Foreign Legion. Mr. Finucane married Miss Mary Gertrude Sweeny on 6-6-1904. F. J. Finucane was the pres. of the Sweeny Investment Co. Finucane was a charter member of the Spokane Club. The original Holley Mason/Finucane building still stands in Spokane located at 157 South Howard St.

The building situates within the Terabyte Triangle Buildings in Spokane. Among early locations of Rossland district, sold by War Eagle Mining Co., of Spokane, controlled by Patrick Clark, John A. Finch, A.

B. Campbell (1845-1912) and others, of Spokane and H. L. Frank, of Butte, White Gooderham & Blackstone syndicate, of Toronto, for $75,000, in 1897. Consolidated Mining & Smelting Co., of Canada later acquired the War Eagle Mine.

Owners of the War Eagle Mine further developed due to the efficiency of electricity. In 1895 P. F. (Patrick Clark) and J. A. Finch contracted together with W. S. Norman (WWP), among others. These associates joined together with the syndicate to organize the Rossland Light and Water Company. [148]

The Le Roi mining Co. in 1910 absorbed into the adjacent properties of the consolidated Mining and Smelting Co. of Canada (known as Cominco Ltd.). The Northport Smelter closed down. In 1929 Cominco closed down the Rossland mines. The Le Roi had produced thirty million during its existence. The Le Roi No. 2 Co., Limited had about 200 acres at Rossland the best known claims were the Josie, Annie and Le Roi Number One; and two also 5 claims in Yrmir district. "The Le Roi mine tours in Rossland, Canada are open to the Public." The Black Bear-War Eagle Gold Mines operated mines in Okanogan County on Palmer Mountain the Mines were headquartered in Spokane, Wash. [149]

May Arkwright Hutton (1860-1915), a well-known Spokane suffrage activist, and her husband Levi Hutton (1860-1928) were partners in the Hercules mine. In 1913 the Custer Consolidated Mining Co. merged with the adjacent Tamarack & Chesapeake Mining Co. forming the Tamarack & Custer Consolidated Mining Co. The latter mine and the Hercules were controlled by the Day brothers, and owned by the Northport Smelter. Jerome Day (1876-1941), Eugene Rufus Day (1873-1922) and Harry Loren Day (1865-1942) served on the board of directors of said mines. The Day's owned a bank and a newspaper company in Wallace Idaho. John H. Wourms (1871-1945) "a lawyer" supervised the legal Department for the Day interests.

W. S. Norman was the president of the Colusa County Quicksilver Mines Co., located in California where his brother Ben had a sheep farm, and sold bottled spring water. W. A. Cummings was the secretary of the Quicksilver Mines, (the company was Spokane based). William S.

Norman, his brother Ben and their cousin William A. Cummings were 'at one time' former residents in the Alpha House/Jenner House located at St., Georges Road England. William Norman was skilled in the art of stenography and worked for his father George as a Reporter/Clerk for the Norman & Cummings Examiner Newspaper Company at 9th Clarence St, Cheltenham, England. George Norman Jr. lived in the Alpha House between the years 1861-1907.

W. S. Norman Secy. and James Cameron Pres. were the chief promoters of the Buffalo Hump Development Co. in 1898. The "Company" was organized to acquire ground in the vicinity of Big Buffalo, Robbins District. Charles Stevenson Sweeny became the pres. of the Federal Refining & Smelting Co. [150]

"Kathleen Francis (Calkins) Beard"

A special thanks, to Kathleen Francis (Calkins) Beard, she was a first and primary source of information for her personal interviews. From memory she added short stories, genealogy, photos, and an oral account of her Great Uncle Benjamin Norman "Birchwood Farm" Kathleen was the grand daughter, of William & Amy Norman.

She was born in Spokane, Washington over one hundred years ago on May 3rd, 1914, the same year her Uncle Ben incorporated the Birchwood Farm Co. Kathleen later passed away on April 5th 2009.

Mrs. Beard was a big part of our inspiration beginning with our first 1989 Birchwood Farm manuscript. The co-authors herein have bequeathed to Museum's, RHMA, MAC, the WSPRC, the Spokesman Review, the Spokane Club and so on, copies of the 1989 manuscript.

When we first met Kathleen we were just beginning to research our rare pair of 1914 BIRCHWOOD FARM COMPANY Stock

Certificates. Doug Olsen a (librarian at the Northwest Museum of Arts & Culture 'at that time') introduced us to Kathleen, a volunteer at the Museum. Mr. Olsen knew Kathleen well. After reading our uncompleted work, Mr. Olsen realized *that our research involved an area at Nine Mile Falls, Wash., where Mrs. Beard lived at* "Birchwood," beginning with her mother, also named Kathleen, who lived there prior. Kathleen and her husband Harold Beard raised their own family at Birchwood within the community of Nine Mile Falls.

.

Mrs. Norman was involved in the Spokane Jr. League, the Terrace Garden Club, and a member of the St. John's Cathedral, being treasurer of both the Spokane Children's orphanage St. Nicholas Guild and the Altar Guild and the Cathedral Landscape Association.

## Acknowledgements
"The co-author's herein would like to express their appreciation; first and foremost; THIS BOOK WOULD NOT HAVE BEEN POSSIBLE without the anonymous individual, dubbed 'Ed,' who gifted us the rare opportunity to write this book, beginning with the inception of two **RARE** antique twin stock certificates. The paper artifacts have proved to be the initial inspiration for the creation of the BFC Grove book. We would like to give Thanks to our dearest family and close friend's, for their patience and encouragement during the writing process! Next we are grateful to all 'the others' who gave us information and access to documents."

References

Washington State Parks and Recreation Commission (WSPRC) "Keepers of Collections" of the Riverside State Park.

The Spokesman Review/Spokane Chronicle for articles and photos, as well as written authorization for letters allowing for a free-flow of information. The Spokesman Review has given us written permission to use stories related to Ben Norman & "Birchwood Farm" in entirety for our Birchwood Farm Company book;

The Birchwood Farm Story, W. S. Lewis, Spokesman Review.

Nelson Wayne Durham Book Trio; Spokane & the Inland Empire, History of Spokane County Washington.

The Articles of Incorporation of the Birchwood Farm Company from Secretary of State-information for authorization written letters.

British Columbia Mines & Corp. - The Copper Handbook, Northwest Mines Handbook Sidney Norman, Rossland Historical Museum and the Famous Le Roi Mine for authorization letters.

The Eastern Washington State University & Historical Societies for information.

Spokane Public Library Downtown Historical Room for photos copies & Info.

The Northwest Museum of Arts & Culture (MAC) for documents.

The Cheltenham Art Gallery & Museum Human History.
The Butte-Silver Bow Public Archives, located at, 17 W. Quartz Street, Butte, MT 59701, for assistance with James Breen facts.

The source content, may consist of free sources; Wikipedia Commons

Researching Cemeteries are a good place to search for surnames & Old Colony Ancestors. "Genealogy" is the study of family lineage and ancestry. Tracing the Walton-Monnette bloodline of descent through continuous intermarriages from their ancestral lines is to numerous to list here, a mere handful of names have been noted.

### Cemetery List:

Kirkpatrick Cemetery Marion Township, Marion County, Ohio:

Anna Dorothy Walton Monnett, David Walton, etc., Kennedy, Foos, Winchell, etc.,

New Caledonia Cemetery, Caledonia Marion County, Ohio

Monnett Chapel Cemetery is in Bucyrus Township, Crawford County Ohio

Chastain (a.k.a. Walton) Cemetery, Eden Township, Section 13, Decatur, Iowa:
Henry L. Walton is buried in the Walton Cemetery noted above:

Oakwood Cemetery Bucyrus Crawford County Ohio:~Monnett & Walton ancestors.
Orra E. Monnette of Marion County, Ohio is a direct descendant of Israel Clark. Mr. Clark's daughter Elizabeth Dey/Day (Clark) Little (1819-1908), has a sworn in affidavit confirming (DAR) Lineage, she is a Daughter of the American Revolution.

Smith Cemetery Marion County, Ohio:
Israel Clark Jr. (1757-1827) Israel served in the Revolutionary war, he met with George Washington.

Powell Cemetery in Eagle Township, Hancock County, Ohio:
Joseph Powell (1760-1835)-(DAR Daughters of the American Revolution)
Joseph Powell and Israel Clark were neighbors in Marion, County Ohio, were later were roommates and young soldiers who served together in the revolutionary war under General George Washington's crossings of the Delaware River.

Mr. James W. Thomas, (attorney) stated; the Crabb family was prominent in Virginia and Maryland that owned a (Bicentennial Farm-200 yrs.) adjoining George Washington in Westmoreland County for two hundred consecutive years (Swan Pond Tract). Jeremiah Crabb, Isacc and Samuel Money (Monet) John, William and Ralph Hileary connected with Alleghany County history early on.

Jacob and Hannah Slagle; The Slagle family visited Gen. George Washington frequently. Jeremiah Monnet m. Aley (Elsie) Slagle

MARION WEEKLY STAR Saturday, March 4, 1905; "Death Ends Suffering of Mrs. Edward Monnette" – Dorothy's remains were taken to Kirkpatrick for Internment.

### Lastly;

There's always more to a story. The evidence herein is based on the study of two "secret" stocks, that which was hidden; exposing a differing account of a collective history. The co-author's purpose in this was to preserve the "Birchwood Farm Company," back-story from going down the "memory hole" - either by disinformation or misinformation – trapped in a web of secrecy. There is still room for ongoing research, "leaving room for improvement".

It has been an honor to write down a brief biography sketch, of Benjamin Norman an Englishman, descended from an old Norman family. Last but not least, acting as secret benefactors, we helped to solve the unknown origin of the mysterious James "Pea vine Jimmy" Walton' not to mention the "other's," territorial pioneers.

We have spent thirty three years (33) of our lives in an ongoing endeavor of unrelenting research, and money spanning (1983-2016/17). As yet, no profits have been earned by the co-writer's text. Hereinbefore manuscripts were bequeathed to libraries and museums; such as the MAC Museum & the Washington State (Parks) for researchers, historians, education, teachers & students alike – in hope of continuing a "free flow" of information of historical significance. 'Come what may' – we are hereby unleashing "BIRCHWOOD FARM GROVE" 2016/17 – for public knowledge and distribution.

More than passing notice should be given to Ben's, Birchwood Farm Company. Lest we forget – attributes of the monuments left behind in honor of our Inland Empire builders, and pioneer "Fathers" for their historical achievements.

All things considered; that's all past tense, we can begin anew path of enlightenment - what lessons can be learned from 'times past,' in the best interest of Society as a whole? (Only) time will tell.

## INDEX - NAMES OF INDIVIDUALS;

"Bone Frenchman"
Boodle James
Bowers H. C.
Boyce Edward
Breen James (Master Metallurgist)
Broadwater Charles (C. A.)
Brooks Henry
Bryan William Jennings
Buckman S. (geologist)
Burch Benjamin Frank Dr.
Burke William and William Hare (Body Killers/Snatchers/Surgeons)
Burnes Cyrus R.
Burnett Charles Compton (Reverend)
Burnett Hugh
Burnett Oswald
Burnett "Percy" (Reverend)
Burnett Sarah Ann
Bush W. George
Prescott George
Calkins Mary Louise
Calkins Harry *Simpson*
Calkins (Norman) Kathleen
Cameron James (Buffalo Hump Pres.)
Campbell Amasa (A.B.)
Christian R. C. (Rosicrucian)
Churchill Winston Sir
Clark Harold
Clark Huguette (the daughter of a "Copper King")
Clark John
Clark F. Lewis
Clark "Patsy" Patrick
Clark Winifred (Winifred Mansion)
Clark William Andrews (Senator)
Clarkson Josephine
Cook Major Aaron
Cone *Spencer* Joseph
Cone Timothy
Corbin Austin
Corbin Daniel Chase (D. C.)
Cowgill Robert P.
Cowley Arthur
Cowley Henry Thomas
Culverwell Fred A. H.
Cummings William
Cutter Kirtland Kelsey

Cyr H. M. St.
Dare Annias
Davenport Louis (L.M.)
Day Eugene Rufus
Day Harry Loren
Day Jerome J.
Daly Marcus
Dennis Graham Barclay
Dickensen John "Founding Father"
Donaghy Lovica
Douglas Thomas (5th Earl of Selkirk)
Drumheller Daniel (D. M.)
Durham Ida (Walton)
Nelson Wayne Durham (N.W.D. trio of books)
Edison Thomas
Edwards Jonathan (Reverend)
Edward Albert (Prince of Wales)
Edward "Ed" (E.T.)
Einstein Albert
Enoch (Spokan Native)
Finch John A.
Finlay Jaco (Jacques)
Finucane Frances John
Finucane Gertrude (Sweeny) Finucane
Foote George (Reverend)
Foote Daniel Sylvester
Foote Francina Harriet
Foote Nathaniel
Foote Stillman
Fotheringham David B. (1st. Mayor of Spokane)
Fuller Samuel Dr.
Fuller Susannah
Garry Chief (Spokane)
Giannini Amadeo Pietro
Gilliam Lane C.
Glover James Nettle (J. N.)
Goodman Frank (B. F.)
Gordon Burgess Lee (B. L.)
Gordon Charles G.
Gordon Raphaelita
Gould Robert Freke (F. G.)
Graves J. P.
Gregson George and Ely (Brothers)
Griffith Thomas Stuart
Haley "Web-Foot Haley" (6 toes)

Hamner Early Henry Jr.
William Hare and William Burke (Body Snatchers)
Hawkins Marjorie (Norman)
Hawkins Mark D.
Hayes Con
Heinze Augustuz Fritz
Henderson Bernice (actress)
Henry IV King
Henry Patrick Sr. (1736 – 1799)
Heron George
Higgins Thomas
Hofstetter John U.
Holmes Sherlock (Sir Arthur Conan Doyle)
Hooker Thomas
Hoover Herbert (Mining Engineer/ later U. S. Pres).
Hopkins Charles (C. B.)
Hunter John
Hurd R. J.
Hutton Levi
Hutton May (Arkwright)
Ide Gilbert (G. B.)
Ike David Vaughan
Insigner Robert
Jenner Edward "the father of immunology",
Jeremiah (Native)
Johnston Henrietta
Johnson Henry
Johnston Henry Drinker Ellis (See Boston Tea Party)
Johnston Martha
Johnston Thomas
Johnston Zua
Joseph Chief
Keller William C. (Keller Store)
Kidd John
King C. B.
Kip Lawrence
Kleinschmidt Albert
Kleinschmidt Reihold
Kleinschmidt John C. (Brother John United Brethren)
Kramer Pete
Lang Margaret M.
Leland Charles E.
Lenhart Henry (Reverend)
Lewis William Stanley (W. S.) "Attorney"
Libenow Ferdinand E.

Ferdinand Francis Libenow
Lawrence George
Ludwig Samuel
Magdalene Mary
Marineau "Al" Albert Alexander (Silver Grill Nuggets)
Marion Doris (nee Giannini)
Marlow A. Thomas
Mather Cotton (Reverend)
Mason Frederick Hamilton
McDonald Finnan
Mitchell Sidney (S. Z.)
Monaghan James
Monnett Augustus
Monnett Jane Ludwig Johnston
Monnett Jean
Monnett Isaac and Pierre
Monnett Orra E.
Monnett Osborn
Monnett Sylvester Frank (Ohio Attorney General)
Monnett Mervin J.
Monnett Mrs.
Monnett Thomas
Moody Henry (H. L.)
Moore Herbert C.
Moore Frank Rockwood
Moore Frederick
Moore Jos. L.
Moore (Sherlock) Sarah Frances
Morgan J. Pierpont (J.P.)
Morgues de Jacques le Moyne
Ness L. B.
Nettleton Julia
Nettleton William (Honorable)
Newberry A. A.
Nimrod Rosella (Gould) ,
Nimrod Strickland
Norman (Sherlock) Aimee Louise
Aimee Norman
**Norman Benjamin**
Norman Emma Mary (Boodle)
Norman George Jr. (Alderman/Mayor)
George Norman Sr.
Norman Honore (Thomas)
Norman Montagu Collet
Norman Sidney

Norman William (W. S.)
Richard Watson Nuzum (Spokane Attorney)
O' Neal Major
O'Farrell Elizabeth O'Grady Marcus (wife of Marcus O'Farrell)
Parker Mary
Parker Sarah
Pettet H. William (W.W.P. agent)
Pike Albert
Poindexter George
Poindexter Miles (Senator)
Post Frank Truman
Preusse Herman
Prickett John
Prickett Jules Lyle
Prickett Louise Elizabeth
Prickett (Sherlock) Marjorie Estelle
Raleigh Sir Walter
Richards J.P.M.
Ridpath William M. (Colonel)
Ripper Jack aka "Jack-the-Ripper"
Rockefeller John D.
Rockwood Cephas L.
Rockwood Sarah Ellen
Roosevelt (Teddy) Theodore (U.S. Pres.)
Rowe George Curtis
Russell E. Antone
Ryan John D.
John E. Savage
(Butler Hotel)
Samuel Wallis
Schumann-Heink Ernestine
Selheim Adolph
Sherlock Dorothea
Sherlock John
Sherlock Rosetta D (Whale)
Sherlock Samuel F.
Sherlock Sarah Francis
Sherwood John Dickensen (J. D.)
Sherwood Josephine Belle
Semmes Dr.
Semmes Raphael
Simms Major
Simon (Native)
Simpson Dr.
Simpson Geddes Mackenzie

Simpson Harry
Simpson Semmes Sir George
Simpson Semmes Raphaelita (N.S.D.A.R.)
Sparling Fred
(Spencer) Anne Elizabeth
Sprague Julian Frank
Steers Louis
Steptoe Edward (Colonel)
Stevens Issac (Ingalls)
Stevens John (Native)
Strickland Robert (R. E. M.)
Stitzel Jacob
Stivers Frank Alexander
Sweeny Stevenson Charles
Thomas Griffith (Glen Tana)
Taylor Clarence L.
Taylor Jacob
Taylor W. H.
Thompson David
Trafford Edward R.
Tsarion Michael (Brian Heatley)
Turbell Francis
Turner George (U.S. Washington Senator)
Tuttle Sylvester (Bishop)
Valkenburg Van Herman A.
Veale Rains Richard (Sheriff of Contra Costa) N.S.G.W.
Diana, Princess of Wales (Frances; *née* Spencer;
Walker Mary D.
Walker Thomas
*Walton Byberry* (Daniel, Nathaniel, Thomas and William) bros.
Walton David
(Walton) Dorothy Annie Monnett
Walton Ellis (Muncy aka Halls Farms)
Walton Elizabeth (Rogers)
Walton George
**Walton James aka Pea vine Jimmy**
Walton Martha (Buffington)
Walton Martin Van Buren
Walton Olivia (Michael Learned)
Walton William C.
Warren Sir Charles (General)
Washington Martha
Waters D. Sidney (Indian Agent)
Weaver family
White Aubrey Lee

White John
White Peregrine
White William (Mayflower Signer)
Wilder Laura (Ingalls)
Wilson Woodrow (U. S. President)
Wilson Oliver (Spokane National Grange)
Winston Alexander Miller
Winston Frances Donnell
Winston George Tayloe
Winston Maria Ellis Norman
Winston Patrick Henry Jr.
Wolter Scott and Janet 74
Worthy Walt & Karen
Wright George (Colonel)
Wright Milton (Bishop)
"Wright Brothers"
Wyatt Anneas (A.J.) "Jews Jack Harp"
Wyatt Sir Francis
Wyatt Thomas
Yantis Benjamin (B. F.)
Yates Francis Dame "Rosicrucian Enlightenment"

Footnotes;

[1] Seattle daily post-intelligencer. June 22, 1883, Image. 1. Ibid, Feb. 2, 1896, Img. 1

[2] London and Its Environs: Handbook for Travelers V. 1889 / Wikipedia

[3] Spokane Daily Chronicle 5-20-1891.  Wikipedia

[4] Nelson Wayne Durham 1912 Spokane (Wash.) Wikipedia

[5] Congressional Series of United States Public Documents, Vol. 2340, Colville Indian Agency, Washington Territory, June 7, 1884

[6] BLM/GLO Accession# WASPAA 009062, Doc# 1537

[7] Spokane Daily Chronicle 5-20-1891

[8] Harvard University, Library Recreation By George O, Shields

[9] The Newport miner (Newport, Wash.) 4-29-1909-1911 Image 7

[10] Register of the Department of the Interior Register 1898

[11] The Wash. Historical Quarterly, Vol. 10-11. / N.W. Durham Vol. 1 pg. 636. / House Documents, Vol. 1; Vol. 4; Vol 266. / W. S. Lewis

[12] Pacific N. W. Qtr, Vo. 39-40. / The Wash. Historical Qtr, V. 10-11.

[13] Spokesman Review/ Historical Records of Washington State

[14] Spokane House State Park in Retrospect / Pacific Railroad Reports, X11, Part 1, 136. The Washington Historical Quarterly, Volumes 8-9

[15] 1884-85 Oregon, Wash. and Idaho Gazetteer and Business Directory, V. 1

[16] Enoch v. Spokane Falls & N. R. Co., Wash.

[17] Duroc-Jersey Swine Record Association 1919-V. 61-pg. 192

[18] U. S. Compiled Statutes, Annotated, 1916: 1916 Vol. 5

[19] Durham V. 1 pg. 462 & Vol. 2, pg. 143. / Bulletin of the Spokane Historical Society, Vol.1, Issue 1 By Eastern Washington State Historical Society Jan. 1917
[20] The Wash. University State Historical Society~The Wash. Historical Quarterly 1917 Vol. 4. / Indian Agent, Benjamin F. Yantis letter to W. T. Gov. Isaac I. Stevens, Native American affairs, May 27, 1857.

[21] Geo. P. Rowell & Co. 1887/ Rowell's American Newspaper Directory

[22] 1904 - An Illustrated History of Stevens, Ferry, Okanogan and Chelan. V. 1. /The Newport Miner, 1-23-1908, Image. 8. / The Colville Examiner, 8-29-1914, pg. 5, Img. 5. / US Fort Colville Accounts Ledger (Pg. 336) Frank Goodman; Business & Finance-Washington-Fort Colville; Feed stores-General stores-Liquor stores-Military depots-Stores & shops-Tobacco shops-Trading posts. The Colville Examiner, Sat. Dec. 16, 1922

[23] History of Lycoming County, Pennsylvania, by John Franklin Meginness

[24] The Colville Examiner, 2-29-1908. Img. 7/ General Land Office (GLO)

[25] An Illustrated History of Spokane County, State of Washington By Jonathan Edwards / History of the Peacock Mine, Adams County, Idaho (MAC)

[26] The Colville Examiner 12-16- 1922. / The Colville Ex. Saturday, December 16, 1922 / Library of Congress / Eulogy The Stevens County Historical Museum preserves the Keller House aka the Keller Heritage Center - Fort Colville Museum,

located at 700 N Wynne St. Colville, Wash. "Death Claims James Walton." Jan. 10, 1908, 5 Img, 5 The Marion daily mirror (Marion, Ohio) 1892-1912 / The Wash. Historical Quarterly Vol. V1. 1923

[27] National archives Ship Roster Passenger list 1851-1852. Wikipedia. (Library of Congress "Death Claims James Walton / Obituary/Eulogy)

[28] A Centennial Biographical History of Crawford County, Ohio 1902 pg. 168 / Wikipedia Commons / Out West, Vol. 30 by Charles Fletcher Lummis 1909

[29] Henrietta daily leader., August 23, 1900, Img 2

[30] History of Crawford County and Ohio: Containing a History of the State of Ohio, pg., 1998., edited by William Henry Perrin, J. H. Battle, Weston Arthur Goodspeed / History of Clermont and Brown Counties, Ohio: Biographical By Byron Williams

[31] Wikipedia

[32] (The Spokesman Review 1925)

[33] U. S. Compiled Statutes, Annotated, 1916: 1916 Vol. 5
[34] Enoch vs. Spokane Falls & N. Ry. Co. 1893 / Durham. Vol. 2, pg. 586

[35] BLM/GLO. / Title Co. Deed Book 65. Filed for HOMESTEAD Application No. 4775, under Section No. 2289, Reproduced/Land National Archives and Records July 2, 1891. The History of the City of Spokane and Spokane County, Washington, Vol. 2, Nelson Wayne Durham, Minnesota **State** university Monkato, Northern Pacific Railway Company. Pamphlet Collection, 1867 - 1967. Land Grants and Land Controversies, 1871 - 1887; Inventory Numbers, 214 - 238: This series is arranged chronologically and includes Debates; Reports of the Senate, Land Commissioner, and House Committee; Decision of the Secretary of the Interior; and Arguments for and against the Land Grants. In addition, this section contains papers related to certain Supreme Court Cases concerning the Northern Pacific Land Grant.

[36] Wikipedia

[37] History of the City of Spokane and Spokane County, Wash. Vol. 2 Durham trilogy of books

[38] An Illustrated History of Spokane County, State of Wash. Jonathan Edwards Pg. 101.

[39] 1911-1912 Water Resources data for Wash, Surface water supply, 1913 part X11
[40] Wikipedia

[41]Washington Water Power Document – Little Spokane River Nine Mile, Mill/Lot 3 - 1889 C. N. Miller/Union Pacific Ry, Co. – (W. S. Norman connection w/ W.W.P.C.)

[42] Durham Vol. page 431 / Spokesman Review April 21, 1957

[43] The Beta Theta Pi, Vol. 23. Mystic Seven Fraternities and Phi Theta Alpha / Spokane Preservation Advocates. *R. Insinger* Director and Attorney / Hubbell's Legal Directory Lawyers and Businessmen By J. H. Hubbell 1907 / Spokesman Review April 21, 1957.

[44] 1896 Biennial Report of the Board of Regents, Issue 4 - University of Washington / Sidney Norman Mines a handbook Vol. 1 / N. W. Durham / S.R. 6-6-1893 / Spokane Chronicle 1-8-1898

[45] Bulletin of the American Institute of mining engineers / Library of the University of Michigan

[46] 1889-1905 N. W. Durham, Spokane's Long Fight For Just Freight Rates, Vol. 1 pages 205, 339, 595-604, 742 / Spokesman Review 1905
[47] The Harvard graduates mag. Vol. 16/San Francisco Blue Book; 1905 Address: Directory / N.W.D., V. 3 / Library of Congress / BLM – GLO

[48] Spokane Cable Railway, the Commercial and Financial Chronicle – pg. 86. 1896.
[49] Wikipedia / Catalogue of the Zeta Psi Fraternity

[50] Wikipedia / Grizzly Bear, January, 1920 V. 26-27 pg 4

[51] U.S. Dept. Of The Interior Bureau of Land Management / General Land Records / An Illustrated History of Spokane County, State of Washington, pg. 529 / By Jonathan Edwards . / The Salt Lake Mining Review, 1916 V. 18

[52] Jonathon Edwards / The Misc. Doc. of the House of Representatives

[53] *The Colville Examiner*. December 16, 1922, Page 6, Img 6 About The Colville examiner. (Colville, Wash.) 1907-1948

[54] 1892 Railway Review V. 32

[55] Jonathan Edwards/ 1916 Trustee for the Spokane Historical…An Illustrated History of Spokane County, State of Washington by Jonathan Edwards

[56] Geography of America, and the West Indies By George Long, A view of religions

[57] Bulletin of Friends' Historical Society of Philadelphia Vol. 2, Number 3, Eleventh Month (November) 1908 pp. 86-90

[58] Now and Then: A Quarterly Magazine of History, Biography

[59] James and Drinker correspondence to the Philadelphia Tea Party (1773-1778)

[60] Biographical Centennial History of Crawford County, Ohio

[61] Wikipedia

[62] Records of the State Enumerations 1782-By 1785 V. 5-6 U.S.

[63] Seven devils 1899 The Mining American-Volume 40-Page 25~Wikipedia Commons / Jonathan Edwards / Site Report - Seven Devils - Idaho State Historical Society

[64] Library of Congress Lewiston Teller. April 8, 1899, Img. 3

[65] Jonathan Edwards / Mines and Minerals Vol. 22
[66] Wikipedia

[67] The Salt Lake Mining Review, 1916 V. 18

[68] Wikipedia

[69] Library of Congress, The Marion Daily Mirror., (Marion Ohio) January 3rd 1908. Another Death Source: The Marion daily mirror. (Marion, Ohio), January 10, 1908, Pg. 5, Img. 5

[70] Library of Congress, The Marion Daily Mirror., (Marion Ohio) January 3rd 1908. Another Death Source: The Marion daily mirror. (Marion, Ohio), January 10, 1908, Pg. 5, Img. 5

[71] Wikipedia, Out West

[72] Book; German Moravian Missionaries in the British Colony of Victoria, Australia ...by Felicity Jensz. / Book; Minutes of the North Ohio Conference of the Methodist Episcopal Church. / By Methodist Episcopal Church. North Ohio Conference 1871. / Detailed Missionary Report. Monnett Chapel / Latimsberville, M. V. Walton / Belle Vernon, James Walton

[73] Wikipedia Commons

[74] 1901 Southern California Quarterly, Volume 5

[75] Idaho semi-weekly world., February 18, 1876, Img 2 (Idaho City, Idaho-Territory_ 1875-1908 / Weiser City Leader, Oct 26, 1888 / The Seven Devils miner-news; Weiser Oct, 26, 1888

[76] HAYS v. WYATT, Idaho, March 1911, pg. 547, Reports of Cases Argued and Determined in the Supreme Court Vol. 19, By Idaho Supreme Court.

[77] The Quarterly, Vol. 5-6 Historical Society of Southern California, Los Angeles County Pioneers of Southern California. / The New North-west., March 26, 1875, Image 3 About The new North-west. (Deer Lodge, Mont.) 1869-1987 / Democratic enquirer. March 26, 1868, Img. 3

[78] The San Francisco call., Feb 21, 1896, Pg 4, Img 4

[79] Congressional Serial Set 1867- 68

[80] Wikipedia

[81] Wikipedia

[82] Ibid

[83] Wikipedia / NWD. V. 2. / The Kinnears and Their Kin: A Memorial V. of History, Biography, and By Martha Humphreys Maltby 1916

[84] Durham V. 1 page. 431 / Spokesman Review April 21, 1957

[85] "The Oregon Native Son" Old Magazine

[86] Wikipedia / Aberdeen herald, Img. 1, Aberdeen herald. 7-14-1910W.T. Official Gazette of the United States Patent Office, Vol. 93, Part 1 / Library of Congress / The National magazine: an illustrated monthly, Vol.

[87] Spokane Title Company / Spokane Court House

[88] Foote family: genealogy and history of Nathaniel Vol. 1 Abram William Foote

[89] Wikipedia / Durham Vol. page. 431

[90] Ibid

[91] Title Co/Auditor's Office

[92] Spokane Historical register/ 12 The Technical world mag. & img. V. X1. March 1909. No.1. / R. J. Hurd bred American Hereford Beef - American Hereford Cattle Breeders Association 1920

[93] Nelson Wayne Durham Vol. 2 pages 130-133 / Seattle daily post-intelligencer., June 22, 1883, Img 1 The Seattle post-intelligencer., February 02, 1896, Image 1

[94] Durham V. 2 pg. 203

[95] Durham Vol. 2 page 354

[96] Assn, Vol. 5-6 N. W. Mining. / N. W. Vol. 1 page 509

[97] Spokane Downtown Public Library Northwest Room

[98] Wikipedia

[99] Ibid

[100] Wikipedia / Huguenots and Jesus of the Languedoc, By Wanda Morisett-Richards

[101] Durham Vol. 1 page 431 / S. R. 2-21-1895 / Nelson Durham Vol. 2 pages 203-205

[102] Kathleen Beard / Spokesman Review

[103] Library of Congress Cataloging in Publication-Data / MAC MUSEUM

[104] Spokane Daily Ch. 6- 13- 1940

[105] Nelson Wayne Durham/ Wikipedia

[106] Ranche and range., March 09, 1899, Page 11, Image 13

[107] Spokesman Review. 2-21-1895 / Spokane Daily Chronicle 5-20-1891 / The Seattle Post Intelligencer 7-11-1890, p. 2, Img.2 / Wikipedia /   Pullman herald., April 01, 1899, Img 6

[108] Engineering and Mining Journal, Volume 111 / Durham Vol. 1

[109] Durham / Spokesman Review / Wikipedia/ The Seattle Republican (1-13-1905) Img 2

[110] Kathleen Beard / Spokane Daily Chronicle 8-18-1933

[111] N. W. D. book trio; / The Northwest Mining Review, V. 1 / Spokane Daily Chronicle 2-27-1892.
1884-85 Oregon, Wash. and Idaho Gazetteer and Business Directory, V. 1

[112] Durham Vol. 2, pg 248.  / Spokesman Review April 21, 1957 / S.R. Nov. 16, 1961

[113] 1905 Engineering and Mining Journal, Volume 79

[114] The National Corp. Reporter, 1917 V. 55...The Hotel World: The Hotel and Travelers Journal V. 89

[115] Journal of Proceedings of the-Session of the National, V. 41-47 By National Grange 1913. / Journal of Proceedings of the National Grange of the Patrons of Husbandry By National Grange 1912 pg. 119

[116] The Tammany Times, Volumes 18-19Messrs. Monnett and Martin, and governor of. Minnesota, and the attorney general of Montana.

[117] Wikipedia
[118] Seven Devil's Rich Mines / Spokane Daily Chronicle – July 10, 1899

[119] Durham / (MAC) Museum

[120] Durham Vol. 1 pg. 475 / Wikipedia

[121] Spokane Title Co.

[122] Spokesman Review / Western Electrician, Volume 6 pg. 284 / Wikipedia

[123] "Sidney Norman" Mining Handbook

[124] Durham Vol. 1 pg. 518 / S. R. 12-26-1959 / Wikipedia

[125] Berg's Personal Hotel Menu / Durham Trio of Books:

[126] British Columbia Mines and corps

[127] (Montvale Farm, Historical Register), documents & letters

[128] Spokesman Review

[129] N. W. D.

[130] Ibid

[131] Wikipedia

[132] "The Royal Union Lodge," No. 246, Cheltenham 1813-1888.  A sketch of its history, compiled from the Lodge Minutes and Contemporary sources by George Norman,
P. M. (Past Master) Illustrated.  (Cheltenham-1888)

[133] Gloucestershire Archives/ Wikipedia

[134] Wikipedia

[135] Ibid

[136] Ars Quatuor Coronatorum: Being the Transactions of the Quatuor No. 2076, London 1186-1888.  Vol. 1. Pg. 15 (George Norman) Pg. 3 –Wikipedia

[137] The Lancet London: A Journal of British and Foreign Medicine, Surgery

[138] Medical Society of London 1843

[139] Spokane Chronicle 4-20-1899

[140] Nelson Wayne Durham; Trio of Books;

[141]  Court House / Rec. S.A.E. Vol. X1.

[142] Wikipedia

[143] Spokane Daily Chronicle, Aug 21, 1916

[144] Spokesman Review

[145] The Journal of Electricity power & gas, Vol. XV11, No. 1

[146] Sidney Norman Northwest Mines Handbook.endnote#  S. Norman & Co. Mining Securities, member of the Spokane Stock Exchange 1918. / Durham

[147] Durham V. 2 pg. 239 / Durham V. 1 pg. 431/Spokesman Review 4-21-1957 / S. R. 3-11-2016

[148] Statues of the Province of British Columbia / Sidney Norman Handbook / S. R. 8-16-1956   Spokane Chronicle 11-01-1984.

[149] Rossland Museum

[150] Sidney Norman Mining Handbook

Made in the USA
Middletown, DE
16 March 2021

35009108R00084